PRESTON HALL
AYLESFORD

To:
The ex-Service People, past and present,
who have made this volume possible.

By the same author:

Aylesford in Old Picture Postcards
1983 ISBN 90 288 2243 7

The Lady Didn't Say
(Under *nom de plume* of Niall Pieters)
1985 ISBN 0 86332 078 3

PRESTON HALL AYLESFORD

by

James H. Sephton

JAMES H. SEPHTON
Aylesford, Kent

Published by James H. Sephton,
496 Station Road, Aylesford, Kent ME20 7QR
First published 1997
Second impression 2009

ISBN 0 9526629 0 6

British Library Cataloguing in Publication Data.
A catalogue record for this book is available
from the British Library.

Designed and produced by DAG Publications,
London. Edited by John Gilbert. Printed and bound by
Antony Rowe Limited, Bumper's Farm,
Chippenham, Wiltshire.

ISBN 978-0-9526629-0-7

9 780952 662907 >

CONTENTS

ACKNOWLEDGEMENTS

The compilation of this work could not have been accomplished without the support and assistance of a number of sources, which are listed in grateful appreciation:

The Kent Archaeological Society's private library in the Maidstone Museum and Art Gallery; the archives of the Royal British Legion Industries; Pamela Haines of Hastings for research into the Brassey family.

The author also wishes to thank the following individuals and organisations for permission to use photographs:

Aylesford Society: Plates 1 (taken by Miss E. M. Glenn), 47
Dorothy Hindbest, cover photograph.
Dorothy Jackson, Plates 46, 48-51, 55.
Maidstone Museum and Art Gallery, Plates 2, 4-6, 9-11, 13, 16-19, 21-3, 32, 41 (E. L. Betts's collection of 1858), Plate 15.
Phillips Fine Art Auctioneers, Plates 7, 8, 27-9 (supplied by The National Monuments Record Centre of the Royal Commission on the Historical Monuments of England).
Royal British Legion Industries, Plates 34-5, 52-4, and line drawings on pages 34, 36 and 76.
West Kent Health Authority, Plates 3, 12, 14, 20, 24-6, 30-1, 33, 36-40, 42-5 (from H.L.C. Brassey's collection of 1904).

Photographs were copied by Ronald White, 24-26 Pudding Lane, Maidstone.

The author also appreciates the invaluable comments from a number of authorities who have read the typescript: Alan McCrerie, President of the Aylesford Society; Alfred King of Wealden Books and of the West Kent Health Authority; Lee McCrea and Martin Hawkins, Authority Secretary, and of the Royal British Legion Industries; Dr Arnold P. Bentley, MBE, MB, BS; Dorothy Jackson; and Doug Scott, Chief Executive.

PREFACE

Aylesford is a place of great antiquity. This is a locality rich in history, legend and romance.

Man's development within a given community is dependent upon the effect of the local landscape and environment. The peculiar geographical situation, with favourable weather conditions, has been a predominating factor in influencing Mankind's establishment and evolution. Sheltered from northerly winds and protected from climatic extremes by the immense outcrop of chalk on the North Downs, Aylesford nestles serenely on a bend of a tidal section of the River Medway.

Much of the record of the past, which we are pleased to call history, is shrouded in the mists of Time. I became intrigued and absorbed in the self appointed task of assembling the available clues in this gigantic jigsaw puzzle, to depict a word picture of the story of Man's local endeavour.

Many people have come to Preston Hall and spent their working lives here. They have found peace and tranquillity in the serenity of their surroundings.

Joy Ingle's little book *Preston Hall – History and Legend* and Ken Wells's mss *Preston Hall and Its Owners* initiated a respect for the past. I became intrigued with the wealth of local history which was not recorded.

This present study contains much hitherto unpublished material. It is preserved as a record for posterity. It is also a dedication to the efforts of those who have settled here and progressed before passing on to the inevitable higher calling.

James H. Sephton

Chapter 1
INTRODUCTION

South of Aylesford village, between the M20 and the A20, ranging over some 220 acres towards the north-west of Maidstone, is the estate of Preston Hall.

The Domesday Book mentions Preston Manor near Malling, suggesting that a dwelling stood here in the 11th century. The termination of the name in 'ton' suggests Saxon origins. The manor was given by Henry I (1100–35) to the monks of the church of St Andrew at Rochester. On Symonson's map of Kent, dated 1596, it was named Preston.

The estate was developed as a farming concern by the Culpepper family as early as the 14th century. By marriage, possession passed into the Milner family. E. L. Betts purchased it during the 19th century. Here he created a sumptuous Victorian country mansion among elegant gardens. It was purchased by the Brassey family, who were generous benefactors to the church and village.

Towards the close of the 19th century, graceful deer grazed over the timbered parkland which extended north to the river. Originally flat meadow formed of alluvial silt, the land sustained elms, chestnuts, ash, larch, oaks and cedars. Many such trees were felled in recent years.

Because of the need for the treatment of wounded troops in 1914, the property became a hospital complex. Together with a small adjacent village, it was acquired by the British Legion. This expanded into a cradle for the support, training and rehabilitation of tuberculous and disabled ex-Servicemen.

Chapter 2
THE CULPEPPER FAMILY

Among the first of this family on record, though by no means the originator, was Sir Thomas de Culpepper of Bayhall in Pembury, Kent, who was Judge of the Great Assize Court in the reign of John (1199–1216). Then followed Sir John de Culpepper. His son Sir Thomas had two children, Sir Thomas of Bayhall and Walter. Sir Thomas had a son John, who was Sheriff of Kent in Edward III's (1327–77) time. His son was Sir Thomas, Sheriff of Kent in 1394 and 1395.

The family separated into different branches throughout Kent. It was Sir Thomas's second son Walter who succeeded to Preston. Walter died in 1327.

The Culpepper arms *argent – a bend engrailed gules* – were carved in several places on the cloister roof of Canterbury Cathedral.

By his wife Joane, Walter was blessed with three sons. Thomas, the eldest, inherited Preston but died without issue. The second son, Sir Jeffrey, succeeded his brother to the estate. Sir Jeffrey was Sheriff of Kent in 1366 and 1374. The third son was John.

Sir Jeffrey left a son William, who succeeded to the estate. His son, Sir John, was a Justice of the Common Pleas in 1406-9. By his wife Catherine he left a son, Sir William, who was Sheriff of Kent in 1427. Sir William died in 1428 and was interred in West Peckham church.

Sir John lived during the reigns of Henry V (1413–22) and Henry VI (1422–61). His son, Sir William of Oxenheath and Preston, had three sons, Sir Richard, William and Jeffrey.

Sir Richard inherited the estate. He had three daughters. The second, Joyce, married Lord Edmund Howard (died 1539) and became the mother of Queen Catherine (1520–42), the fifth wife of Henry VIII (1509–47).

The estate passed to Sir Richard's younger brother William, whose son and heir was Edward. He was interred in 1533 in the chancel at Aylesford near to his mother Margaret.

Edward's son and heir was John, who had a son Thomas (1517-87). On the accession of Queen Mary in July 1553, Thomas joined the rebellion with Sir Thomas Wyatt the Younger (1521-54). Consequently, the estate of Preston was presented to Mr Cartwright, the Deputy Sheriff.

Thomas Culpepper was confined in the Tower of London. He had a fellow prisoner in Thomas Vane, who had married Thomas's cousin Elizabeth Culpepper. They appeared to have been Protestant martyrs, as suggested by their inscription on the stone wall of their cell:

'Be thou faithful to the end and I will give you a crown of eternal life — 1554, T Fane, T. Culpeper, of Ailsford, Kent.' (This is a misquotation of Revelation 2, 10.)

They were pardoned and Fane lived to become Sir Thomas Fane of Mereworth Castle. The estate of Preston was restored to Thomas Culpepper, who later became a Revenue Commissioner. In 1561 he was Purveyor of Rochester Bridge.

Two labourers, John Mylles and Isaac Frenche, with the latter's wife Agnes, were indicted for grand larceny before Judges John Southcote and Thomas Gawdy at Rochester Assizes on 19 March 1579. On 11 October 1578 the indicted broke into the house of Thomas Culpepper at Aylesford and stole twelve table napkins (valued at 5s), eighteen table napkins (4s), two tablecloths (4s), two long towels [value omitted], a pair of sheets (2s) and a pillowbar (16d) belonging to Thomas, and three smocks (3s), two aprons (2s) and a kerchief (6d) belonging to his daughter Anna. On 31 October 1578, at St Margaret's, Mylles and Isaac Frenche, of St Margaret's, stole a carpet (20s) and a tablecloth (2s) from Henry Lane. Mylles and Isaac Frenche were found guilty and allowed clergy. Agnes Frenche was found not guilty.

Thomas's daughter Anna married Henry Crisp, the fourth son of Sir Henry Crisp. An inscribed brass was inserted in the floor between the central piers of the chancel of the parish church at Aylesford:

'HERE LYETH THE BODIE OF HENRY CRISPE THE FOVRTH SONNE OF SIR HENRY CRISP KNIGHT. HE HAD TO WIFE ANNE YE DAVGHTER OF THOMAS CVLLPEPPER OF AYLESFORD ESQVIRE. THEY HAD ISSVE FYVE SONNES AND ONE DAVGHTER. HE DIED THE SECOND OF DECEMBER 1594.'

This brass plate, measuring 15 in x 4.75 in, was screwed into the wood of a 19th–20th-century parquet floor, suggesting that it may have been removed from its original position.

Thomas Culpepper's (1517–87) second son was also named Thomas. He married Marie, Thomas Pinner's daughter. He was the last Culpepper to hold the fortified manor of Old Soar, Plaxtol, built in Kentish ragstone in 1290 by Culpepper of Preston. William of Preston died possessed of it in 1326. By 1601 Thomas had sold it to Nicholas Miller for £2000. Nicholas was the richest member of a local family originating from yeoman farmers of the 15th century.

In 1604 Thomas purchased from James I (1603–25) the tenure by ancient demesne of the royal manor of Aylesford. He became Sir Thomas and inherited the estate.

Against the east gable and under the central piers of the chancel of the parish church at Aylesford was erected one of the finest rectangular tomb chests in Kent. This well-preserved monument of Elizabethan style, supported the life-size recumbent effigies of a knight and his lady. It was in grey alabaster mottled with veins of iron oxide (dimensions in Appendix 3). The black paint on the lower of the two steps of the marble plinth was flaking away. Below the architrave the long north and south sides were divided into three equal bays. The east and west ends were each of one bay.

Surmounting was the effigy of a bearded bare-headed knight in black armour edged in gilt. His bare hands were clasped together in an attitude of prayer. After the Netherlandish fashion introduced during Elizabethan times, he lay on a rush mat with rolled-up ends, on one of which rested his saboton heels. He wore rowel spurs. Contrary to tradition, there was no canine effigy at his feet. Probably, this was because he was a farmer, not a soldier.

On his left was his lady. Her hands were similarly clasped together. Both effigies were orientated with the feet pointing eastwards. Under each head was carved a cushion with piped edges, gilt brocade on the upper surface, and heavy tassels at each corner.

The lady wore a plain white dress draped from the neck and tucked in concealing her feet. A plain white shawl was pleated over the head and cascaded below the knee. The absence of jewellery was particularly remarkable. The rather sombre nature of the lady's apparel was in contrast to the ostentation of her husband.

An inscription on the west end of the monument recorded:

'HERE LIETHE INTOMBED SR THOMAS COLEPEPER KNIGHTE, BY BLOODE & DESCENTE DESCENDED OF MANY WORTHYE ANCESTORS: IN HIS LIFE TIME FOR HIS WORTH AND DESARTE BELOVED OF ALL MEN: & IN HIS DEATH AS MVCH LAMENTED & BEMONED: HE HAD BY DAME MARIE HIS ONLY WIFE AT THE TIME OF HIS DECEASE THREE SONNES & TWO DAVGHTERS: WHICH DAME MARIE TO PERFORME HER LAST DVTY IN REMEMBRANC OF HER FAITHFVLL LOVE TO HER DECEASED HVSBAND AT HER OWNE COST ERECTED THIS GRATEFVLL MONVMENTE: VNDER WHICH HE RESTETH AND BY HIS LIVELY FAITHE HOPETH A JOYFVLL RESVRRECTION. HE DIED 12 OCT: 1604.'

This monument was embellished with armorial bearings in colour of six coats quarterly;

1) *Argent, a bend engrailed gules* (Arms of Culpepper).
2) *Argent, a chevron sable between nine martlets gules* (Arms of Hardreshall).
3) *Gules, on a cross argent five escallops of the first.*
4) *Barry of four, vert and gules, three bezants, two and one in chief a cross formee or.*
5) *Gules, seven mascles, three, three and one, or.*
6) *Sable, a fesse chequy argent and sable between three owls proper, impaling azure a chevron argent between*
   three lions' heads erased, ermine crowned or.

The Culpepper crest was *a falcon volant argent, belled or.*

A large undecorated floriated armorial device on the east end was obscured by the close proximity of the column of the east wall of the chancel.

In the central bay of the south side were carved effigies of three kneeling sons, viz. William, Richard and Thomas. In the corresponding bay on the north were similarly displayed carved effigies of three kneeling daughters, viz. Francisca, Maria and Ann.

There is an anomaly concerning the effigies carved on the

sides of the monument, and the text of the inscribed tablet on the west end. This was probably the original stone commemorating Sir Thomas's interment in 1604. Dame Marie was probably pregnant when her husband died, such that the birth of the third daughter, Ann, was posthumous.

The imposing monument was commissioned after 1604 by their eldest son, Sir William, to commemorate not only his father but also his mother. The original simple tablet pertinent to his father, of dissimilar stone, was incorporated into this later design.

There was no evidence on the monument to identify the sculptor. An inset of stone 2 in square on the south cornice may be a later attempt to erase his signature. However, the style in Dame Marie's effigy resembled that of Lady Elizabeth's black and white marble tomb chest in All Saints Church, Hollingbourne. Lady Elizabeth was wife to Sir Thomas Culpepper of Greenway Court. She died in 1638 and was interred in the Culpepper family vault beneath the chapel at the east end of the north aisle of All Saints Church. Lady Elizabeth's monument was the work of the sculptor Edward Marshall (1578-1675). His signature was incised on the top moulding of the west side of the plinth.

E. Marshall was employed by the Culpepper family to create two delightful memorial brasses at Ardingly, Sussex. Elizabeth, baptised in Bolney on 20 November 1627, died aged seven years and was interred on 8 December 1634 at the side of her grandmother, Dame Elizabeth, who died in 1633.

On the death of Sir Thomas of Preston Hall in 1604, the estate passed to the eldest son William. He was created a Baronet in 1627 by Charles I (1625-49) and became Sheriff of Kent in 1637. He had three daughters, Alicia, Francis and Helen.

Alicia was married at Aylesford to Sir Thomas Culpepper of Hollingbourne, by licence of the Prerogative Court on 31 December 1663. A daughter Frances was baptised on 20 February 1664. Dame Alicia died on 20 April 1731 aged ninety-three, and was interred in St Mary's Church, Lenham. A daughter, Margaret, wife of William Hamilton of Chilson, died on 9 October 1736 aged seventy, and was similarly interred at Lenham.

After the death of her father, Sir William, Baronet, Francis married John Alchurn, of Boughton Monchelsea on 25 April 1667, by licence of the Court of Faculties.

Helen was interred at Aylesford on 22 October 1667.

Sir William's brother, Sir Richard, Baronet, of Preston Hall, had several children by his wife Dame Margarett. A son William was interred in the parish church at Aylesford on 16 March 1658. Sir Richard, Baronet, was similarly interred at Aylesford on 10 January 1659. A son Richard was interred on 10 January 1660. A daughter, Helene, was interred on 10 December 1661. The widowed Dame Margarett was interred on 26 September 1691.

Two children survived their parents. One was a daughter Alicia who was born *c.* 1657, and the other was Sir Thomas, who in 1704 succeeded to the title and the estate.

Sir Thomas became Sheriff of Kent in 1704. His wife was Dame Elizabeth. She was interred in the parish church at Aylesford on 5 February 1708. Sir Thomas, the last Baronet of the line, died without issue. He was interred on 24 May 1723 in the family vault beneath the south chancel of the parish church at Aylesford.

His sister Alicia was the last of the line of Aylesford Culpeppers. She inherited the estate of Preston Hall.

There were many families in Kent and Sussex called Culpepper, with a variety of spellings, viz. Culpeper, Colepeper, Colpepper, etc. Some families were isolated, but others were integrated by marriage. Ardingly, Aylesford, Bayhall, Bedgebury, Greenway Court, Headcorn, Hollingbourne, Maidstone, Oxenheath and West Peckham have all produced this name.

The firstborn son took his father's or his grandfather's Christian name. Thomas was the most frequently occurring name. William was almost as common. The second son was named William and the third Richard. The name John was also favoured. The occurrence of the names Jeffrey and Walter was sparse.

Joanna, Jane and Anne or Anna, Elizabeth, Margareta or Margarett were popular among the women. Marie or Maria, Alice or Alicia were also favoured.

Thus, one Christian name may have been used simultaneously in more than one branch of the family.

The frequent occurrence of otherwise innocuous family names has created a great deal of confusion amongst historians and has produced errors in identification. The family tree in Appendix 1 will elucidate the Aylesford branch of the Culpeppers.

14

Chapter 3
THE FORMER PRESTON HALL

Towards the close of the 18th century there was an avenue extending in a direct line from Aylesford's 14th-century bridge south through parkland to Barming. Flanking this avenue were beautiful established specimens of the cedars *deodora*, *libane* and *excelsa*.

Isolated cedars survived into the 20th century in open parkland between the distribution depot of United Carriers and Aylesford cemetery. Between the workshops of the Royal British Legion Industries (RBLI) and the mansion were the remains of a retaining wall with a corner of the former avenue. Bushes followed the course of this avenue. Some cedars stood along the drive from the south porch of the mansion to the A20 Maidstone to Larkfield road. Further cedars survived to the west of the RBL bungalows in Hermitage Lane.

To the north and below the later mansion, and close to Home Farm Cottage, was the site of the former Elizabethan manor. It was located on the west of the cedar-flanked avenue.

This early structure was a plain white stucco square building of an elegant appearance. On the east was a portico over the entrance. Tall chimney stacks may have been in brick.

This manor was demolished on 19 August 1848, when the estate was in the possession of E. L. Betts. A clock was salvaged and presented by him to Aylesford parish church, where it was installed on the tower's south face.

Salvaged from the demolition was a bronze bell 15 in high, 17.5 in diameter across the rim, and 9 in diameter across the top. It was originally mounted on a wooden beam. The bell bore the inscription:

'Dame Hellen Culpepper of Alsford in Kent 1662.'

Together with another bell it was preserved during the late 1970s in an iron safe in a locked chamber accessed from the tunnel beneath the later mansion.

Of the original Elizabethan manor, only a large barn retained its former character at the close of the 19th century. The north gable was constructed in ragstone to a height of *c.* 6 ft 9 in. This height decreased along adjacent sides. Above the ragstone courses of the north gable, the wall was built in brick. Carved in the stonework of a window frame in this gable were the initials 'T.C.' and the date '1102'.

The barn's south gable was similarly in brick on a stone foundation. The upper course of the masonry was slightly above ground level. In the south gable was a stone window frame without inscription.

The four corners of this barn had ragstone quoins. Above the level of the upper ragstone course of the foundation, the sides were boarded up to the eaves. Two gables on the east probably formed the entrances. The original inscribed crumbling stone window frame in the north gable was incorporated by renovation into the north wall of a later farm building. The remnants of this structure were demolished during 1977 to clear the area for redevelopment. During 1978 new warehouses were erected on the site. They were occupied by a firm of woodware importers and merchants trading under the name of Arthur Heath & Company, with TNT Inter County Express, a transport business. The site of the north wall of the original barn may be estimated by inference. The fragments of the original inscribed stone window frame from the north gable were removed to the grounds of T. W. Kemsley's home at Seymours Hall Place Farm, Barming.

Close to this barn was formerly an elegantly styled oast house built entirely of brick, with stone quoins. This building has long since been demolished. On the left-hand stone portal of the doorpost giving entrance were incised the date '1102' and the initials 'T.C.' carved twice, once with the shield which bore the arms of Culpepper only and again with a shield on which the heraldic device was quartered with the arms of Hardreshall. A similar date and initials were carved on a chimney piece. The Hardreshall arms, *argent, a chevron sable between six martlets gules*, were carved in several places on the cloister roof of Canterbury Cathedral.

The initials 'T.C.' were presumably those of Sir Thomas

16

The Culpepper monument in Aylesford Church

The south facade of Preston Hall in 1858

The south facade of Preston Hall in 1904

The southern approach to Preston Hall in 1858

The sout-west prospect in 1858.

The original south door of Preston Hall in 1858

A carriage before the original south door in 1870

The main portico on the south in 1887

Above: The Orangery from the south in 1858
Below: The Orangery from the north-east in 1858

An internal view of the Orangery in 1858

The prospect from the Orangery towards the east in 1904

The north-west prospect in 1858

Above: The Hall from the north in 1904
Below: The Hall from the north in 1905

41554. Aylesford: Preston Hall. F.F.& Co.

The North Terrace and Fountain from the south-west in 1858

The prospect from the Terrace towards the north- west in 1858

The Fountain in 1858

Culpepper, the son of John Culpepper. The quartering of armorial bearings did not occur before c. 1326. The arabic numeral figures of the date 1102 were not in common use before the 13th century. The authenticity of the carved date 1102 has therefore been disputed by historians.

Sir Thomas Culpepper (c. 1350) married Elizabeth, daughter and heir of Sir John Hardreshall. This Sir Thomas Culpepper was therefore the first who could use the arms of Hardreshall quartered with his own. He succeeded his father in the manor of Bayhall in Pembury, and there kept his shrievalty in 1394 and 1395.

The initials 'T.C.' and the date '1102' probably represented Thomas Culpepper (1517-87) who married Margaret Culpepper, daughter of Thomas Culpepper of Bedgebury in Goudhurst, lineally descended from the Culpeppers of Bayhall, as the builder of the barn and oast house in 1582.

Alternatively, his son Sir Thomas, who married Marie, the daughter of Thomas Pinner, may have built the barn and oast house in 1602. This was the Sir Thomas who died in 1604 and was commemorated by the tomb chest in the chancel of the parish church.

The architectural style of the demolished barn and oast house was typical of 16th-century work. Considering the inscription on the door frame of the oast house, the initials 'T.C.' with the single Culpepper arms suggest the father, Thomas Culpepper (1517-87), and the initials 'T.C.' with the quartered arms could have been attributed to the son, Sir Thomas Culpepper (d. 1604).

Therefore, the date 1102 incised on both the window frame in the north gable of the barn, and also on the chimney piece and the left-hand stone portal of the door-post of the oast house, may be interpreted as representing the year 1582 or more probably, 1602.

During the late 1970s an allegorical representation in oils of the original Elizabethan manor hung on the east wall of the reception area which was the former atrium of the later mansion.

A line engraving entitled *Preston Hall in Aylsford, the Seat of Sr Thomas Colepeper Bart*, dated 1719, from E. Hasted's The *History and Topographical Survey of the County of Kent*, Vol. 4, 1798, depicted the former estate around the Elizabethan manor. There were several copies of this engraving. One was in the mansion's reception area which was the former atrium. One, presented to Dr A. P. Bentley MBE, MB, BS on retirement from the National Health Service in 1986, was in the manager's office of the RBLI. A third was displayed in the Hengist Restaurant, 7-9 High Street, Aylesford. This engraving was published as a rear plate by the RBLI in 1975 and 1977, in two of their brochures celebrating The Legion's 50th anniversary.

Chapter 4
LADY ALICIA TAYLOR

About 1675, Alicia Culpepper married Herbert Stapeley Esquire, the son and heir apparent of Sir John Stapeley, Baronet, of Patcham in Sussex. Herbert was MP for Seaford in 1679. They were blessed with several children, all of whom died young. Herbert, the fourth son, died in 1687 aged three and was interred in the chancel of Folkington Church, Sussex. Alicia's husband, Herbert, died *c.* 1690.

The widowed Alicia Stapeley remarried. Her second husband was Sir Thomas Taylor, Baronet, (1657–96) of Park House, Maidstone. The ceremony took place at St Peter's Church, Ditton. The parish register recorded:

'1692 Oct 6 Sir Thomas Taylor of Maidstone, Baronet, and Madame Alicia Stapeley of Aylesford were married.'

Sir Thomas died in 1696. Their son Thomas (1693–1720) succeeded to the baronetcy at the age of three.

Lady Alicia Taylor, being left a widow for the second time, was again wooed. She married her first cousin, Thomas Culpepper, a barrister, the second son of Sir Thomas Culpepper of Hollingbourne. Lady Alicia continued to reside in Park House, Maidstone, where she brought up and educated her son, Sir Thomas Taylor. Her third husband died young. Their son, Sir Thomas, died in 1720 aged twenty-seven. The baronetcy became extinct.

Lady Alicia's brother, Sir Thomas Culpepper of Preston Hall, died in 1723 without issue. His baronetcy became extinct. She therefore inherited the estate. (Their genealogy is elucidated in the family tree in Appendix 1 relevant to the Aylesford branch of the Culpeppers.)

In need of a partner to share in the management of the estates, and someone to comfort her in old age, she remarried. Her fourth husband was Dr John Milner MD of Pudsey, Yorkshire. The marriage ceremony was solemnised at St Peter's Church, Ditton. The parish register recorded:

'1723 Oct 16 Dr Millner of Maidstone and the Lady Taylor of Aylesford were married. Lady Taylor, the last of the Culpeppers, had no children.'

Lady Alicia settled all her estates, including Preston Hall, on Dr Milner and his heirs, reserving only her life interest. John Milner devised the inheritance of the estate of Preston Hall to his brother Dr Charles Milner MD.

Following the pattern established by her previous husbands, John Milner did not survive the union with Lady Alicia. He died in February 1724.

In her lonely, childless widowhood, Lady Alicia lived on at Preston Hall. When she died in April 1734, she must have been nearly eighty. The entry for her interment was entered twice in Aylesford's parish register. She was interred in the north chancel of the parish church.

Chapter 5
THE MILNER FAMILY

After Lady Alicia's death, Dr Charles Milner resided at Preston Hall. He survived to a good age, dying unmarried in 1771. Charles Milner acquired Sir Robert Faunce's endowment lands and property. For preaching on St Swithin's Day, the incumbent at Aylesford received 10s annually from Charles Milner. A sum of not less than 10s was distributed annually by him to the poor.

By his will, dated 4 April 1766, a sum of £20 was provided annually from 160 acres of land in the parish, to be paid to a schoolmaster appointed by the owner of Preston Estate, to educate poor children in Aylesford. The school room was above the south porch of the parish church of St Peter and St Paul.

In 1833, a plot of land in Boling Alley was purchased from a local blacksmith, James Kemsley, for £115. This acquisition provided for the building of a modest school for boys. It was extended in 1840 to include a girls' school. In 1872, it was enlarged. Half the cost was met by public subscription, the remainder being donated by H. A. Brassey. This school was known as Aylesford St Peter's Church of England Primary School, Mount Pleasant.

By his will, Charles Milner's estates passed to his nephew, the Rev Joseph Butler. He changed his surname to Milner in 1771, to facilitate inheriting the estate. He was appointed Rector of St Peter's Church, Ditton, in 1769. He was also Rector of Burham. He retained both livings until his death in 1784.

Joseph Milner resided at Preston Hall, which he modernised and almost rebuilt. He took down a high wall which had stood before the manor house. With great taste and considerable expense, he laid out the adjoining grounds. Some features of this garden landscaping, viz. the avenue of cedars, survived as late as 1990.

In 1772 Joseph married Sarah. She was the daughter of the Rev Stringer Belcher, Rector of Ulcombe. Sarah's mother was Sarah, daughter of Justinian Champneis, Esquire, of Boxley. Joseph died childless on 26 July 1784, aged fifty-four. He was interred in the north chancel of the parish church at Aylesford on 5 August 1784.

Sarah died on 27 September 1803, aged seventy-two, and was laid to rest alongside her husband.

The estates passed to Joseph's nephew, Charles Cottam of Farningham. In May 1788 he assumed the name Milner, and in 1791 married Miss Harriett Dyke, youngest daughter of Sir John Dixon Dyke, Baronet, of Lullingstone Castle in Kent.

They were blessed with eight children. Harriet Philadelphia was born on 6 December 1792 and died on 27 June 1793. Charles Joseph was born on 10 August 1796 and died on 6 September of the same year. Mary Ann was born on 13 March 1799 and died on 5 June 1836. Harriett Sarah was born on 19 September 1800 and died on 31 May 1802. Charles was born on 16 September 1801 and died on 19 September 1844. Caroline Elizabeth was born on 2 July 1802 and died on 28 January 1843. John was born on 4 February 1804 and died on 6 October 1846. Henry Robert was born on 29 January 1805, the youngest and last surviving child.

Their mother, Harriett, died in August 1808.

In 1811, Charles built a road from Aylesford bridge to the London Road. This was named Park Road, and later Hall Road. He built a cottage at the junction of Park Road and the London Road. He also provided land to widen the road from Aylesford to Mill-hall. This was Water Lane, and later Station Road.

Charles died on 7 January 1836, aged seventy-two.

Preserved among the archives of the Health Authority at Preston Hall during the late 1970s was a vellum document, dated 1842, which was the original copy of indentures of the estate in the name of the son Charles (1801-44). Henry Robert Milner enlisted in the army on 7 February 1822, aged seventeen. He joined the 94th Regiment in 1828 where he saw continual service in the Mediterranean, Ceylon and the East Indies, until the return of the regiment from Madras in June 1854. As colonel, he commanded the regiment for fourteen years, and was employed on the staff of the Madras Army for five years as Brigadier commanding at Aden, Cannanore and Bangalore.

Being the last surviving relative after October 1846, he arranged to sell his estate in 1848 to Edward Ladd Betts.

In his fiftieth year, with the rank of Major General, Henry Robert died at Plymouth on 14 January 1855. Under the tower of

Aylesford's parish church, on the south wall of the baptistry, was an incised marble tablet erected to his memory. He was interred with his ancestors in the family vault below the north chancel. A semicircular arch in the east external gable was built in 19th-century red brick with random ragstone filling. This was the final seal of this vault. (The family tree in Appendix 2 elucidates the Aylesford branch of the Milners.)

Chapter 6
THE BETTS FAMILY

Edward Ladd Betts was born at Sandown, Kent, on 5 June 1815. Under his father's direction, he began his career as a railway contractor. He built the Black Rock Lighthouse near Beaumaris as agent for Hugh and David McIntosh. At the age of eighteen, he had sole responsibility for the construction of Dutton Viaduct on the Birmingham to Warrington railway line, as agent for David McIntosh under Joseph Locke. After the successful completion of several railway building contracts in England and Wales, he entered into partnership with Sir Morton Peto, and built many railways at home and abroad. In 1843 Betts married Ann, the youngest daughter of William Peto. She was born on 19 September 1820. They were blessed with two children, a daughter Elizabeth Peto who was born on 22 October 1846, and a son Percy Campbell who was born on 7 January 1856.

A portrait of E. L. Betts was exhibited at the Royal Academy in 1844. It was painted by J. Dowling, a fairly obscure artist, described as a miniaturist who exhibited at the Royal Academy between 1839 and 1872.

Sir Morton Peto built a sumptuous Jacobean mansion at Somerleyton, Suffolk, in 1844 with John E. Thomas (1813–62) as his sculptor and architectural draughtsman. Thomas is best known locally for his sculpture of Queen Victoria in Maidstone High Street, for the striking equestrian sculpture of Lady Godiva donated by Mrs Thomas to Maidstone Museum and Art Gallery, and for the statue of *Apollo and Daphne*, formerly in Brenchley Gardens, Maidstone, before removal in January 1991 after being vandalised.

Encouraged by his partner's initiative, Betts decided to imitate. In 1848 he purchased the Preston Hall estate from Henry Robert Milner, and demolished the former manor house. On a slight eminence of clear ground to the south, he created a mansion.

Building commenced during the 1850s to the designs of Thomas. Betts reputedly brought labour from Belgium for the work. The building was completed by 1857. This date was recorded on the weather vane.

E. L. Betts commissioned an infants' school near the 14th-century bridge, for the education of his workers' children. This school was erected in 1853 by E. W. Stephens of Maidstone. It was later named Aylesford St Peter's Church of England Primary School, Brassey Annexe (Infants). The adjoining building, 'Rosalind's Cottage', was renovated in 1865 by E. L. Betts. He provided a similar school at Ditton.

Betts was Magistrate and Deputy Lieutenant of Kent, and High Sheriff of Kent in 1858.

During the 1860s, in common with other contemporary businessmen, he became involved in the gamble which followed a speculative era, and came to financial difficulty. The entire estate of slightly more than 2,810 acres was sold by Daniel Smith, Son & Oakley, 10 Waterloo Place, Pall Mall, at auction in Tokenhouse Yard, London on 17 June 1867. It was purchased by Thomas Brassey, Betts's associate in several railway construction enterprises. Betts left Preston Hall in 1867. His firm of Peto-Betts & Crampton failed in 1868.

The residents of Aylesford wished to perpetuate Betts's memory. By public subscription, a memorial fountain, supplied by Mr Cowdy of London, was erected in the playground on the west of the Brassey Annexe school. The inscription stated:

'This fountain was erected A.D. 1868, to commemorate the many acts of kindness conferred on this parish and neighbourhood by Edward Ladd Betts Esq., of Preston Hall, by whom this school was erected and the village supplied with pure water.'

It was officially opened by the Rev Anthony Grant in April 1868 and was removed *c.* 1928. Only the commemorative sandstone plinth survived. The last few words of the inscription were missing.

In an attempt to restore his failing health, Betts visited Egypt in 1871. He died at the Old Cataract Hotel at Aswan on 21 January 1872, aged fifty-six. His remains were brought back to Aylesford for interment.

25

Against the exterior of the south chancel wall of the parish church was a pink granite monolith. Before the priest's door into the chancel was a flat stone inscribed:

'ENTRANCE TO VAULT.'

Beneath this stone were steps leading down into the family vault. Here were interred E. L. Betts, his wife Ann who died on 23 January 1908, Elizabeth Peto who died on 1 March 1940, and Percy Campbell who died on 14 October 1878. (The family tree in Appendix 4 elucidates the Betts family.)

Chapter 7
THE BRASSEY FAMILY

Thomas Brassey was born at Buerton, Cheshire, on 7 November 1805, the son of John Brassey, farmer, of Bulkeley, Cheshire. Thomas was educated at Chester Grammar School. At the age of sixteen he was articled to a surveyor named Lawton of Chester, with whom he later went into partnership. He acquired fame as a successful civil engineer and railway contractor. He was involved in over 170 contracts for the building of railways, docks and sewers. He built 33 per cent of all the railway track in the British Isles and much of the French railways. He was responsible for creating 5 per cent of the total mileage of the world.

In 1831 he married Maria, a daughter of Joseph Harrison of Birkenhead. They were blessed with four sons; Thomas, John who died in infancy, Henry Arthur and Albert. Thomas, the father, suffered a severe attack of bronchitis following the opening of the Fell railway in 1867. In 1868 he suffered a paralytic stroke. He recovered, but in consequence dragged one leg. He died at St Leonards on 8 December 1870, aged sixty-five, and was interred in the churchyard at Catsfield. He left some £5,000,000 to his wife and three surviving sons.

The eldest son, Thomas, was born at Stafford on 11 February 1836. He married Anna Allnutt in 1860. They were blessed with a son and four daughters. One daughter died at the age of six years. Thomas was Liberal MP for Hastings between 1868 and 1886, and Mayor of Bexhill 1907–8.

For several years they lived at Beauport Park near Hastings. His father built a house for them at Normanhurst Court, Catsfield, Sussex, in 1865–70, which became their home in 1878. The family retained the house and grounds, although it was used by St Hilary's Girl School in 1922. The property sustained considerable damage due to military occupation in 1939-45, and was demolished in 1951. Some of the masonry was salvaged and reused in Pulpitt Gate, a pseudo-Tudor house at 76 All Saints Street in Hastings Old Town.

The Brassey Institute in Claremont, Hastings, was erected in 1878-80 to the design of W. L. Vernon for Thomas. In Venetian Gothic Revival style, it was in red brick with dressed stone details. The roof was tiled with a truncated spire. The windows were mullioned with leaded glazing. The four storeys and basement accommodated a museum, a reference library, an assembly room, the school of art and science, with a private suite for Thomas when he was MP. Accommodation in the basement adjoining a club-room was provided for the Hastings rowing club, but was not used by the club. The Institute was presented to the town on 9 June 1888, by Thomas, together with the reference library. The Institute was the first home of the Hastings Museum.

Thomas and Anna neither owned nor resided at Preston Hall. Always an enthusiastic and capable amateur yachtsman, he achieved international acclaim from world cruises with his family between 1874-1918 aboard the *Sunbeam*, a three-masted topsail schooner of 334 gross tons fitted with an auxiliary compound steam engine. She was designed by St Clair J. Byrne and built by Bowdler, Chaffer and Company of Seacombe, Wallasey, in 1874 of composite construction. She was registered at Liverpool. Anna is remembered for her fascinating books of their voyages in the *Sunbeam*.

He was knighted in 1881. He was Civil Lord to the Admiralty (1880-3), and its Parliamentary Secretary (1884-5). He wrote *The British Navy* (1882-3), a major work on British naval history, and founded the yearbook *Brassey's Naval Annual* (1886). On the resignation of William Gladstone in 1886, his services to the Admiralty were rewarded with a peerage. On 16 August he was created Baron Brassey of Bulkeley, Cheshire.

A few days after *Sunbeam* left Port Darwin, Australia, on a cruise, Lady Anna died, on 14 September 1887. She was buried at sea.

Baron Brassey married Sybil de Vere Capell, daughter of Viscount Malden in 1890. They were blessed with one daughter.

In later life Baron Brassey held several important public appointments. He was President of the Institution of Naval Architects (1893-5). He was Governor of Victoria, Australia, (1895-1900) and Lord Warden of the Cinque Ports (1908-13). On 5 July 1911, he was created Earl Brassey and Viscount Hythe, of

Hythe, Kent, by George V (1910–36). Earl Brassey died on 23 February 1918 in London.

After an eventful career under several successive owners, the **Sunbeam** was sold in 1929 to Thomas W. Ward Ltd, who broke her up at Morecambe Bay in 1930. Her restored gilded wooden figurehead was formerly on display in the Callender entrance in the east wing of the National Maritime Museum at Greenwich. She was represented by a builders' model on the upper floor of the Durbar Hall in Hastings Museum and Art Gallery, John's Place, Cambridge Road.

Because Thomas, the father, spent much of his time abroad on railway construction, he appointed two of his sons, viz. Henry Arthur and Albert, together with Henry Arthur's wife's brother-in-law, Robert Mitchell Campbell, as trustees of the estate of Preston Hall.

Henry Arthur was born on 14 July 1840. On 24 June 1866 he married Anna Harriet Stevenson, daughter of Major George Robert Stevenson of Tongs Wood, Hawkhurst. She was born in 1845. They were blessed with three sons; Arthur Albert was born on 4 March 1868 and died on 1 January 1869. Henry Leonard Campbell was born on 7 March 1870. Harold Ernest was born on 29 March 1877.

Following the death of his father Thomas in 1870, Henry Arthur came to the estate of Preston Hall, which had been purchased for him by his father. The estate of Heythrop Park, Chipping Norton, was similarly purchased for the younger son Albert.

Henry Arthur built a school in Pratling Street for the education of the children of his pottery workers. Miss Emma Cole taught a mixed average class of fifty children. This school closed in 1905. The premises were converted into two cottages, which were demolished in 1967. In 1877 he built St Mark's Primary School Church of England at Eccles. Miss Taylor was the teacher in 1902.

Sunday school treats and sports days were held every summer in the park at Preston Hall. At Christmas, the Brassey family visited the school to present prizes for the best work and the best recited catechism. The Brassey family presented oranges, boots for the boys and items of clothing for the girls.

29

He was MP for Sandwich 1868-85, and High Sheriff of Kent in 1890. A County Survey of Kent in 1873 listed him as the owner of Preston Hall with 4,060 acres 3 roods 20 sq poles at a gross estimated annual rental value of £10,577 0s.

The gross value of Henry Arthur's personal estate at his death on 13 May 1891 was £1,075,913 with the net value at £1,042,611. The executors to his will were his brothers Baron Brassey and Albert with Robert Mitchell Campbell. Anna received £8000 per annum for life with the use of his town house, furniture and £1000 worth of plate at Bath House, Piccadilly.

Four additional rooms were added to the Hospital of the Holy Trinity, or the almshouses, with similar materials in a manner compatible with the original. Over the entrance was a stone plaque with a magnificent representation of the Brassey heraldic devices and the inscription recording the erection to the memory of Henry Arthur and endowed by his son Henry Leonard Campbell in 1892.

In the north-west of the churchyard of the parish church was an imposing monument over the family vault of Henry Arthur and Anna who died on 15 July 1898. Delicately carved in fine marble was a statuary group comprising an allegorical representation of an angel comforting his sorrowing widow. The monument was formerly surrounded by a bronze palisade. He and his wife were commemorated by a brass plaque on the wall of the south nave of the church near the pulpit, and a fine memorial window at the west gable of the north nave.

The second son, Henry Leonard Campbell, survived to inherit the estate. He was educated at Eton and Christ Church, Oxford. He held commissions in the 3rd Battalion (Royal Sussex Militia) of the Royal Sussex Regiment in 1890-3 and the Queen's Own West Kent Yeomanry in 1893-5. He was appointed Justice of the Peace for Kent in 1893.

On 30 June 1894 he married Lady Violet Mary Gordon-Lennox, the second daughter of the 7th Duke of Richmond and Gordon. They were blessed with six sons, four of whom were born at Preston Hall. Ronald Henry was born on 21 May 1895 and died eight days later. Cecil Henry was born on 3 October 1896. Gerald Charles was born on 28 December 1898. John Leonard was born in 1903 and died on 9 March of the same year.

Henry Leonard Campbell stood successfully as a Parliamentary candidate in the Conservative interest for Cambridgeshire East in January 1903. He was appointed Justice of the Peace for Northamptonshire in 1904.

Lady Violet held Preston Hall in great contempt, referring to it as the workhouse, being fit only for commoners. It was a newly created property with no historical legacy. Doubtless, she was devastated and distraught by the loss in infancy of not just one, but two sons. She may have been disturbed on learning the fate of a former occupier, viz. Lady Alicia Taylor, whose four husbands and the children from three of them, all suffered an early death. Lady Violet, being wealthy in her own right, was not unreasonable in urging removal to another residence.

Henry Leonard Campbell acquired Apethorpe Hall, Northamptonshire in 1904, which became their family home. To please Lady Violet, he disposed of his Preston Estates mainly to tenant farmers and those who had lived or worked on the estate. The public houses 'The Bush' and 'The Lower Bell' were sold to Style and Winch. The indenture, dated 18 April 1904, included the sale of 'The George Inn' and 'The Pottery Arms'. He sold Church Farm and the sandpit on the north of the parish church of St Peter and St Paul in 1906 to his fellow churchwarden, Silas Wagon, the sitting tenant. Lower Tottington and 'Anchor Farm' were sold to J. J. Chambers and Thomas Danes in 1906. The entire estate, comprising well over 4000 acres, was sold for a total of £250,000.

The management of 'Rosalind's Cottage' and St Peter' Church of England Primary School, Brassey Annexe (Infants) was secured by the formation on 1 July 1905 of the Brassey Trust. This was a means of perpetuating the memory of his family by providing financial support for the Church of England in Aylesford. It was administered by the incumbent and churchwardens, and, when necessary, by co-opted members.

Henry Leonard Campbell and Lady Violet Mary were blessed with two further sons. Bernard Thomas was born on 15 February 1905, Peter Esme on 5 December 1907.

Henry Leonard Campbell stood successfully as a Parliamentary candidate in the Conservative interest for Grantham in January 1906. He was High Sheriff of Northamptonshire in 1907. He was

MP for North Northampton from January 1910 to November 1918. He served in the First World War in the Northampton Yeomanry 1914–17, and 1917–20 in the Territorial Reserve. He was MP for Peterborough Division from December 1918 to May 1929. He was Deputy Lieutenant of Northamptonshire in 1922. He was created a Baronet on 29 November 1922, and raised to the peerage as the first Baron Brassey of Apethorpe on 26 January 1938. His wife Lady Violet Mary died in 1946. He died in a London nursing home on 22 October 1958, aged eighty-eight years.

Cecil Henry died 11 September 1949. Gerald Charles was commissioned as Lieutenant in the Coldstream Guards. He was killed in action on 27 August 1918.

Their fifth and surviving son, Bernard Thomas, was knighted and became the second Baron Brassey of Apethorpe. He died on 28 June 1967. In succession, his son, David Henry, became the third Baron.

At the commencement of the twentieth century, the heraldic devices of Sir John de Grey of Codnor and his son Sir Henry, John Sedley of 1605 and H. L. C. Brassey, dated 1892, were painted on one of the glass windows in the north aisle of the parish church of St Peter and St Paul. This window was transferred before *c.* 1917 to a mullioned light in the chapel of the almshouses at Trinity Court, Rochester Road. During the renovations of 1986-8, it was removed to the community room. (The family tree in Appendix 5 elucidates the Aylesford branch of the Brasseys.)

Above: The Fountain with Running Water in 1858
Below: The Fountain with Running Water in 1904

The west prospect in 1858

The Garden to the west in 1858

The path from the North Terrace in 1858

The arbour on the North in 1904

An arcade of roses in 1904

An internal view of the Entrance Vestibule in 1904

The Atrium c. 1887

The Great Hall c. 1887

The Billiard Room c. 1887

The Study in 1904

Above: The Library in 1904
Right: The marble fireplace in the Dining Room in 1858

The Lodge by the South Gate in 1904

The Lodge by the West Gate in 1904

The Laundry in the south-west of the Estate in 1904

Chapter 8
THE NEW PRESTON HALL

The twin lines of cedars between Barming and the mansion were very impressive. Yet, they were not entirely original. One tree felled in the 1950s was planted in 1851. Another tree which fell in the storm of 1987, and lay recumbent until 1993, was planted as a five-year-old in 1851. These dates were derived from dendro-chronology, or tree-ring dating, which is a precise dating method using the annual growth of rings in trees.

Barming station was originally called Preston Hall. The name was changed at the insistence of the Brassey family. The main entrance to the estate remained from the south. The main A20 road encompassed former parkland from east to west. A long brick wall marked the south perimeter.

Originally, the south approach road into the grounds was domi-nated by two masonry pillars, surmounted by stone urns, which sup-ported ornate wrought iron gates. This entrance was replaced before 1866 by two rusticated Caen stone pillars, surmounted by stone spheres, on each side of the drive. Suspended from iron ball caps on the central pillars across the drive was a massive pair of ornamental wrought iron carriage gates. Between each pair of pillars on either side of the drive was a similar but narrow gate for pedestrians.

The iron gates have long since disappeared. The central pillars were removed after 1950 in the process of facilitating the passage of modern vehicular traffic. The easternmost pillar collapsed from its plinth. Its stones were abandoned in a confused jumble behind the wall. By 1996 the westernmost pillar alone remained intact.

In June 1962 a fine plaque designed by Hillary Stratton was erected near the main gates, bearing the words:

'PRESTON HALL CHEST HOSPITAL.'

The name subsequently changed, and the plaque was replaced by a simple sign in cerulean lettering:

'PRESTON HALL HOSPITAL.'

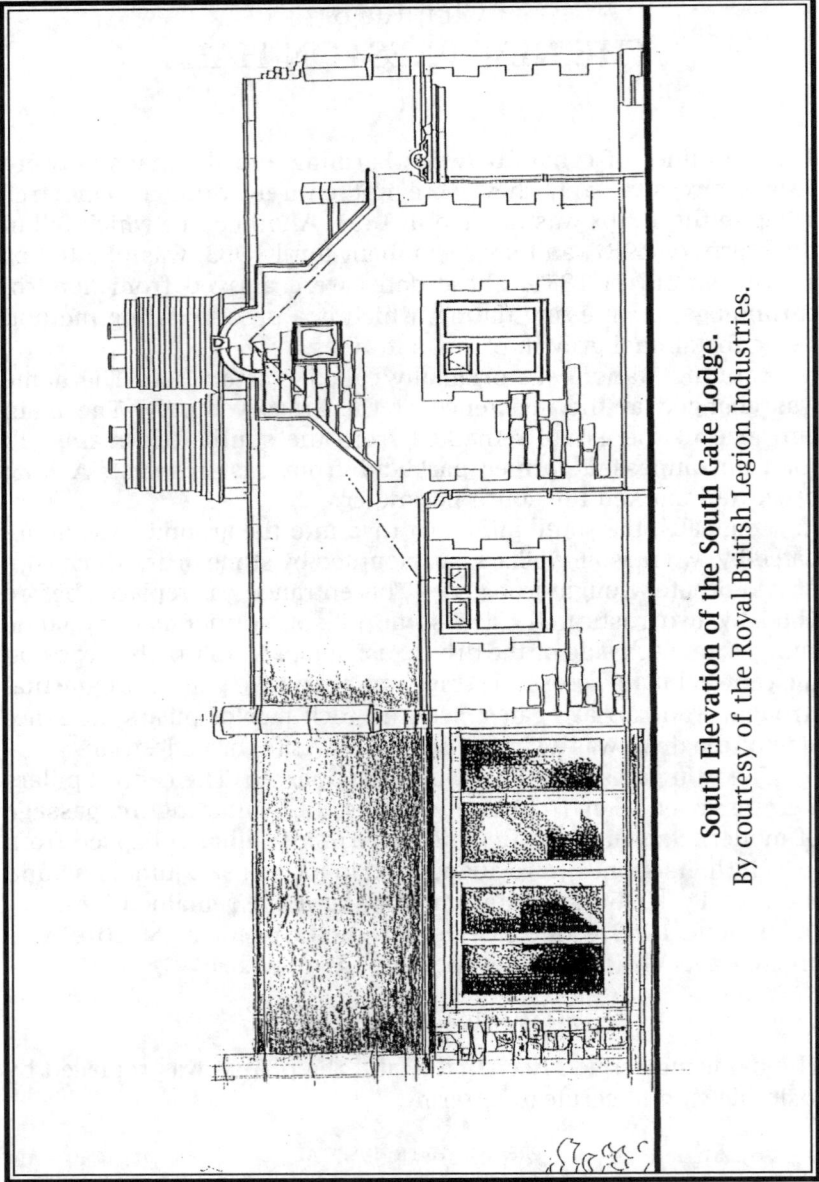

South Elevation of the South Gate Lodge.
By courtesy of the Royal British Legion Industries.

On the west of the main gateway and snug behind the perimeter wall stood the south gate lodge. This single-storey structure was in regular courses of rusticated Kentish ragstone with Caen stone quoins and white painted Caen stone door and window surrounds. Heraldic devices over gable windows were heavily corroded. The lodge had a slate roof and tall brick chimney stacks. This abandoned derelict property was boarded up at the doors and windows for a number of years.

A west gate lodge in ragstone, thatched with reeds, stood at the approach to the mansion through a shrubbery drive. An east gate lodge was built in the style of the half-timbered houses of an earlier period.

The former gravel drive of the cedar-flanked avenue between the main road and the mansion became a 300-yard stretch of macadam-surfaced road with foot pavements bordered by multifarious flower beds. The trees and shrubs along these borders were planted shortly after 1948.

On either side of the inner gate to the courtyard on the south was carved statuary. On the west a lioness fondled her cubs. On the east a male lion wrestled with a boa constrictor. In Italian marble on a massive pedestal of Portland stone, J. E. Thomas represented *Peace* and *War* respectively. Originally, these statues were on either side of an arbour to the west of the northern terrace. A wooden corral fence on either side of the drive near these statues was removed in July 1980.

Hand-made wrought iron gates at the entrance to the inner courtyard were provided by H. A. Brassey. They were removed after 1904. The iron pintles remained in the masonry.

In Kentish ragstone embellished with bold Caen stone dressings, the mansion was symmetrical about the south entrance porch. It was dominated by a central tower between complex shaped gables, and three bays extending the full height of the gables. The lower part of the tower was enriched by double rusticated pilasters with carved capitals supporting moulded trusses. These carried a heavy cornice and ornamental balustrade. The tower had a fine open-worked corbelled parapet with angled pinnacles. The tower's flat roof was surmounted by a flagstaff and weather vane. Fine mullioned bay windows adorned all sides of the mansion. The southern facade was

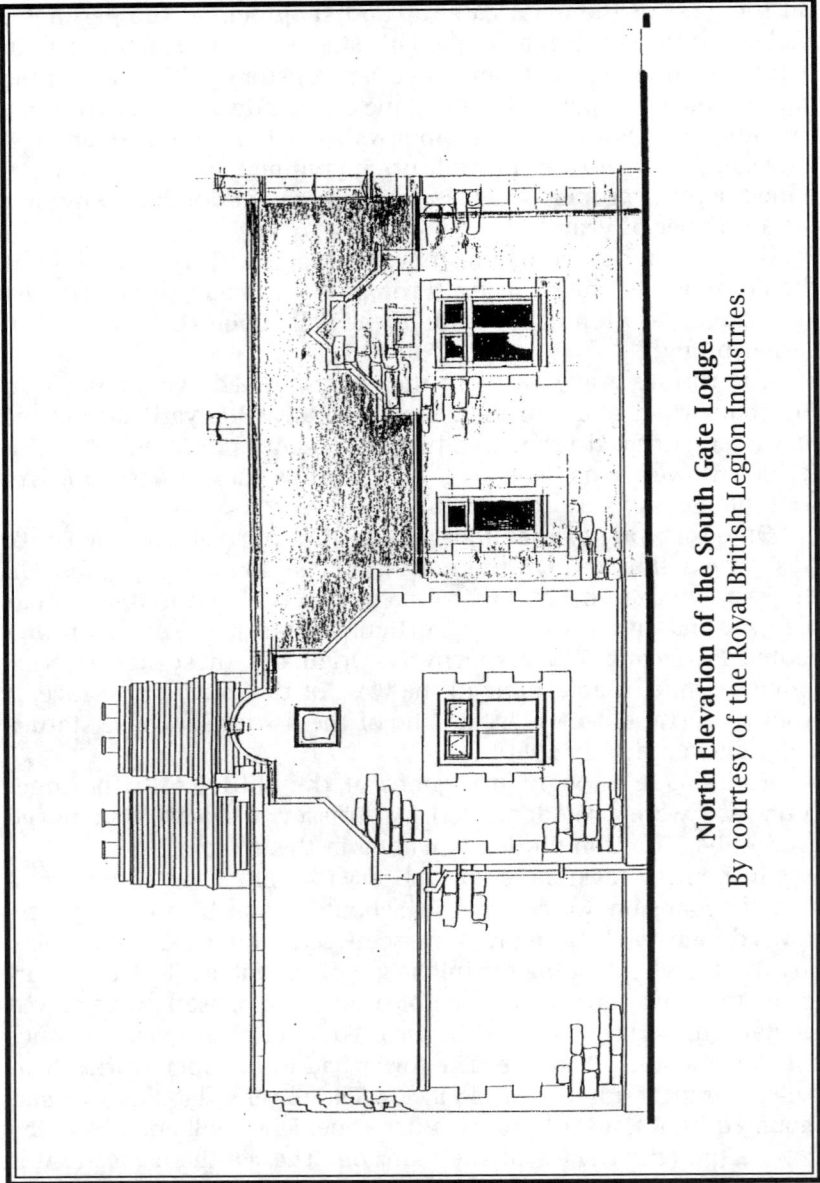

North Elevation of the South Gate Lodge.
By courtesy of the Royal British Legion Industries.

relieved by a delicately moulded oriel window at the west end. The building was listed as one of architectural and historic interest.

There was a turret with cupola on the end of the east wing. A long service wing on the west accommodated the bachelor stable and gardening hands. It was divided by a lofty archway called the 'Bothy'. Above this arch was a clock turret. The clock bore the name of the maker, James Gill, of Maidstone. Originally a cupola and weather vane dominated this arch, but the cupola was removed for safety reasons during the early 1950s. Numerous pinnacles on the roof of the mansion were removed at this time, as their occasional collapse presented a safety hazard.

Beyond, and at right angles, was a range of coach houses in rusticated ragstone. Converted into garages, they retained their original slate roof. The stable was a single-storey structure between west and east gables in regular courses of rusticated ragstone with Caen stone quoins and window surrounds, with a shallow slope to the slate roof. In the stable yard was the horses' granite drinking trough with centre drain. The former mounting block was removed to permit the passage of vehicular traffic.

Towards the close of the 19th century the mansion was clad in creepers. A large magnolia tree dominated the south.

The roof was slated with ornamental ridging. Kentish ragstone, random coursed and rustic faced, was the predominant building material. Window frames, quoins, open balustraded parapets, and dressings were in Caen stone. The architectural style was Renaissance Gothic, reminiscent of the late 16th century.

The greater part of the external embellishments was achieved in soft stone. Due to the effects of atmospheric pollution, this had eroded. Heraldic devices have deteriorated to become almost unrecognisable. The outer stonework was cleaned and restored during 1958–9. Consequently, the fabric assumed something of its original noble character. Early in 1980, the south facade was again cleaned by a contract firm of specialists. The masonry was restored by inserting new stone in part.

Along the north of the mansion was a gravelled terrace 270 ft by 12 ft wide. There were grass slopes and two flights each of eleven stone steps leading to the flower garden to the north. A shorter flight of steps terminated the west of the terrace.

Below the terrace was a large central fountain carved in Portland stone by J. E. Thomas in 1851. A large tazza vase, surrounded by four Tritons, was supported on a lily stem. Originally, the fountain was surmounted by two stately Sicilian marble life-size effigies of *Acis and Galatea*. By 1904 these effigies had been transferred to Brenchley Gardens, Maidstone. Surrounding the fountain were crescent-shaped flower beds, forming a delightful rose garden, and edged with low box hedges laid out by Nesfield. During the 1950s, the hedges were removed.

A relative of a former owner presented two exquisite pieces of garden sculpture in the form of white marble portraying children at play. They remained concealed for a number of years until *c.* 1960. They were placed on the terrace north of the great hall on either side of the stone steps leading down to the fountain. This sculpture was decapitated by vandals.

Edged by a formal limestone balustrade, the north terrace swept around the east corner. Here formerly stood an orrery, a device for astronomical measurements. The stone plinth and restored pedestal remained, yet the orb disappeared during 1979. Overhanging the ruined balustrade on the north-east corner of the north terrace were some of the ancient ilex or holm oak.

At the turn of the 19th century, the view north from this terrace comprised mainly parkland richly endowed with trees, and an occasional glimpse through the foliage of the North Downs.

On the north-east corner of the mansion was formerly an orangery. It was octagonal in plan with lofty glass dome, arched plate glass doors and windows, and was paved in York stone. It lapsed into neglect and decay after *c.* 1904. Its twisted ironwork and broken glass constituted a hazard. It was demolished in 1953, but the foundations remained. The entrance lobby to the orangery was converted into a kitchen annexe on the north-east of the subsequent staff dining-room.

The main entrance to the mansion was by an imposing portico on the south. This was erected *c.* 1880. It was supported by pairs of columns on substantial bases with rusticated panels. Over the porch was a balustraded parapet. Two fine griffins, one at each corner, commanded the view south. Both effigies deteriorated severely due to the effects of atmospheric pollution. The keystone over the front door and under the porch was carved by J. E. Thomas into a representation of a bearded head.

Entry was by means of a pair of polished oak doors with plate glass panels. These doors opened into a vestibule, 15 ft square. On the marble mosaic floor was a leopard-skin rug at the turn of the century. A recess on either side contained marble statuary. Life-size figures of *Psyche* and *Flora* were by B. Spence of Rome. Elegant furniture created a sumptuous impression. Stags' antlers sprawled over the arch to the inner door. Here was an inscription:

'Welcome the Coming, Speed the Parting Guest.'

To the east was a cloakroom 13.5 ft by 8 ft. A lobby and water closet to the west was converted into a modern telephone switchboard. A pair of oak doors from the vestibule opened into the atrium or staircase hall, 34 ft by 25 ft, paved with marble. It extended to the height of the mansion, and was crowned at the summit with the dome of a large and richly ornamented lantern light. From the north was formerly a grand double flight of oak staircases ascending to the west and east to square half-landings. Each staircase terminated in a gallery supported on ornate trussed cantilevers along the south. The staircases were 4 ft 6 in wide. Massive banisters surmounted carved perforated sides and terminated in massive panelled newels supporting bronze gas lamps. The natural gas was produced in a special plant near Home Farm. Fitted by Messrs Strode, this contained three retorts and two gas holders containing *c.* 8000 cubic ft.

The single grand oak staircase and balustrade in the southwest corner was a survivor of the original pair. The gallery along the south was extended by similar connecting galleries along the west and east. A heavy oak and mahogany balustrade followed the entire length of the balcony.

The walls were formerly relieved by pilasters and arcaded openings which assisted in lighting the corridors surrounding the atrium on both the ground and first-floor levels. These openings were accentuated by elongated architrave columns, and gilded Corinthian capitals. These arcades have been sealed. The architrave columns and Corinthian capitals disappeared in later austere decoration.

At the close of the 19th century the principal attraction of the atrium was three fine tapestries made at the Royal Tapestry Works, Windsor, for H. A. Brassey:

1. ***The Battle of Aylesford*** , AD 455, made in 1879 by E. M. Ward, RA (1816–79). This tapestry (24 ft by 13 ft) depicted an allegorical representation of the dramatic climax of the combat between Horsa and Catigern. Horsa lay supported by his comrades, while in the middle distance were personal aides holding the reins of the terrified steed of the fallen warrior.
2. T***he Men of Kent marching at the head of Harold's Army to meet Duke William at the Battle of Hastings 1066 AD***, made in 1879 by J. E. Hodgson, RA.
3. ***The Battle of Rochester Bridge***, made in 1880 by J. E. Hodgson, RA.

These three tapestries were purchased by private subscription and presented to the Maidstone Museum and Art Gallery *c.* 1937. ***The Battle of Aylesford*** hung in room A at Maidstone Town Hall. ***The Men of Kent*** was stored in Maidstone Museum. ***The Battle of Rochester Bridge*** hung on the staircase at Maidstone Town Hall.

At the north of the atrium was the great hall, 32 ft by 21 ft. Corbels supported the carved oak timbers of the lofty vaulted roof. This supported a fine panelled ceiling by Mr Place of Grays. The upper lights of the north bay window contained eighteen panels of modern stained glass by Ballantine of Edinburgh. A massive chimney piece represented Hengist entertaining Vortigern. The lower aspect of the walls was richly panelled in oak. The walls were embellished with armour and swords. There was a narrow arched doorway leading into an upper balcony in each southern corner to form the minstrels' gallery. These, and the oak wall panelling, were removed after 1918.

To the east of the great hall was the withdrawing-room or dining-room, 30 ft by 24 ft, with a spacious bay window. The white ceiling was embellished with birds, vine leaves and acorns. The fine statuary marble chimney piece by J. E. Thomas was exhibited at the Great Exhibition of 1851. This piece displayed a medallion of Chaucer with alto and bas-reliefs with figures of ***Dorigine*** and ***Griselda.***

On the north of the far east wing, fairly high up, were the initials 'A.H.B.' which probably represented Anna Harriet Brassey. Over an internal window was a heraldic device. Over a pantry window was the initial 'B'.

Sliding doors separated the withdrawing-room from the music-room, 20.5 ft by 19 ft. The two windows commanded a side view of the orangery. The fine statuary marble chimney piece by Thomas was exhibited at the Great Exhibition of 1851. The figures represented *Una and the trials of Florimel.*

During the autumn of 1959 the Hospital Management Committee undertook the interior decoration of the larger ground-floor rooms. The coffers of the atrium were painted a warm dark red, to contrast with the white moulding and cool green of the surrounding wall. A floor was inserted into the great hall, reducing its height. The original ceiling survived in the upstairs room subsequently used as a boardroom. The former wall between the great hall and the dining-room was removed. The ground-floor area was greatly increased to accommodate the subsequent cafeteria or staff dining-room. Modern colouring replaced the dark paint of former years. The new ceiling in the cafeteria was painted pale grey, with the walls lemon.

A south-facing room, adjacent to the subsequent telephone exchange, remained unchanged since the turn of the century. This may have been the former library, 20 ft by 17 ft. A significant quantity of oak carving survived. Richly appointed carpentry loomed up to the original ceiling. Internally, and above the door, was an original painted panel by Owen Jones. (This is not listed in Appendix 6.)

Adjacent, and also facing south, was the morning-room, 20 ft by 18 ft, which may have been used as a study.

To the west of the great hall was the gentleman's room, 21 ft by 17.5 ft. This was used as a schoolroom and later as the doctors' dining-room. Four panels of modern stained glass in the upper lights of the north bay window survived down to 1996. On the door was a heraldic device with initials. This was a relic of E. L. Betts. There was a secret door into a fire-proof room of ragstone and fire brick. Up to the 1970s, this small room contained a Chubb quadruple iron safe. This room became a pantry with a new door leading into the subsequent dining-room.

To the west of the gentleman's room was the billiard room, 32 ft by 24 ft. The noble recess window commanded the terrace view. This room was designed and built by Banks and Barry. The embellishments were by Mr Place and Messrs Crace. A massive chimney piece was in Greotte marble. An elaborate system of gas lighting provided illumination.

Giving access to the upstairs bedrooms from the gallery above the south of the atrium was a narrow wooden staircase. Along the sides were finely panelled doors for wall cupboards. Inside were shelves intended to store brass vessels used for hot water for bed-warmers. The doors could not be opened because of the provision *c.* 1960, of handrails down each side of the staircase. A barrel-vaulted plaster ceiling displayed stucco representations of trailing plants.

In the north-east corner of the first floor was the boudoir, decorated in sea green relieved with gold. There was an elegant statuary marble chimney piece.

The main bedroom was magnificently panelled in oak. Various plants were represented in the carvings, viz. briary, fritillary and pomegranates. Finely carved lions' heads formed bosses along the cornice. On the internal door were carved the initials 'E.L.B.' representing E. L. Betts, and 'A.L.B.' representing his wife Ann Ladd Betts. A heraldic device carved between them carried the motto:

'Ostendo non ostento.'

On translation, this became:

'I show but without display.'

A private staircase in Caen stone with ragstone case led to the domestic accommodation on the upper floor.

Towards the close of the 19th century, the mansion contained a choice collection of paintings, which were subsequently removed. (These are listed in Appendix 6.) There was some noble statuary by B. Spence and J. E. Thomas, inside the mansion and in the grounds.

Apart from the principal rooms described there were five main bedrooms, eleven secondary bedrooms, two secondary dressing-rooms, two nurseries, eighteen servants' bedrooms, four bathrooms, eleven WCs, housekeeper's and butler's sitting-rooms, together with the kitchen, 23 ft by 21 ft, paved with Yorkshire stone, scullery, larders, pantries and extensive domestic offices and cellarage.

Throughout the mansion were a number of hidden doors concealing stairs. These descended to the basement tunnel paved in Yorkshire stone extending the entire length from west to east. A tunnel exit was on the west and another on the east. Here were several adjoining chambers illuminated by gas lighting; and here was the bakehouse with patent oven by Powell. One chamber was the wine cellar, and another was part of the kitchen facility. The equipment for the original hot-air piping, by which the principal rooms were heated, was located in this tunnel. Some stairs were subsequently commissioned as fire escapes. The entire complex was later used for various engineering services.

There were three lakes. One was created to the left of the front entrance to the mansion. A larger lake was sited by the railway to the north. To the south-west of the estate was an artificial lake built *c.* 1855 by E. L. Betts. He created an exotic Japanese garden. Tall trees and flowering shrubs sheltered the lake perimeter. Water was supplied by pipe. Traces of this were still visible during the early 1940s. Stones skirted the water's edge, and reeds grew along the margins. There was a small ornamental stone bridge. The lake was stocked with fish. Sometime after 1945, the lake was cleared of weeds. One of the workmen inadvertently put his foot through the clay deposit forming the lake's foundation. The water drained away into the subsoil. A tree grew through the centre of the stone bridge, causing it to collapse. This beautiful garden has long since succumbed to the housing development of the Royal British Legion Village (RBLV).

The former ice-well was situated to the east of the mansion where a high grassy bank sheltered the insulated dome from warm southerly winds. It was converted *c.* 1928–30 into an electricity sub-station.

To the north of the grounds was an extensive range of greenhouses. Many exotic foreign plants were imported by the **Sunbeam** and propagated under glass before planting out in the grounds. A greenhouse, 44 ft by 16 ft, survived north of the early brick wall which separated RBLI Supplies Department and Clark Mews. It was later demolished to permit redevelopment for the RBLI. Along the north side of this wall were ragstone and brick workshops and sheds which survived down to 1996.

On the north-west of Rochester Road (B2011) at Tottington, amidst sheltering trees, lay a natural spring deep in a ravine. Several sarsens were scattered around the spring head. Most were submerged by the surrounding artificial pond. The discharge formed a stream linking a number of ponds known as the Fish Ponds. Several sarsens could be found along the water-course. This was a site of great antiquity and significance. Spring water from Tottington supplied Aylesford's domestic demand during the 19th century. Water was supplied free of charge. This spring was part of the Preston Hall estate. A pump at Home Farm supplied a cistern on an upper floor of the mansion.

After an alternative supply became established by the Mid Kent Water Supply in October 1953, the spring at Tottington become neglected and overgrown. Water from here continued to supply the greenhouses until their demolition.

Some traces of the walls of the kitchen garden remained to the north of the estate in the 1940s when Bert William Kemsley (1879–1955) was cultivating the ground.

Further north was Home Farm Cottage in ragstone with Caen stone dressings and a half-timber elevation above. There was a quaint gabled porch, dormer window and tall Tudor-style chimney stacks. The cottage contained twelve rooms and excellent cellarage. The cottage was occupied by Thomas W. Wall in 1902. Adjacent were detached oasthouses. The adjacent barn and the west wing of the stables were destroyed by fire during the early 1970s, but the east wing survived.

Sheltering amidst trees on the west of the estate was the badminton or racquet court. This roofed building, 60 ft by 30 ft, in white brick was ornate with a towering turret on one corner. There were blank walls *c.* 25 ft high lined with Roman cement. There was a spectators' balcony. The floor was asphalted. There was a cast-iron water tank, 35 ft by 20 ft, on the flat roof. Fed by pump from Home Farm, this tank supplied the garden and mansion offices. Three trefoil arched windows at the west survived.

To the south-west of the estate, near the artificial lake, was the keeper's cottage. Random ragstone walls with brick facings supported a gabled tiled roof. Tall brick chimney stacks projected above the ragstone breasts on each gable. Over the rustic entrance porch was a dormer window. Some six rooms were contained. Around the cottage was a perimeter wall in random ragstone.

A laundry was built to the south-west of the grounds to provide an essential household service. This structure had rusticated ragstone walls with dressed stone quoins and window surrounds. The tiled roof had a variety of gables. Tall brick chimney stacks of Tudor style towered above. The structure was sheltered by stately established trees. During the early 1930s it was completely destroyed by fire. It was demolished to facilitate the housing development of the Duchess of Kent Court for the RBLV.

The Brassey family loved Richmond Hill, located near the top of Holt Hill. It was probably named after Lady Violet's family name. Among planted flowering shrubs was a summer-house, octagonal in plan and called 'The Holt'. A circumventory verandah and balcony were built in logs. It had a round roof of Kentish thatch. By 1904, the ragstone walls were partly clad in creepers. H. L. C. Brassey and Lord Cornwallis often met there for breakfast after an early morning ride over their respective estates which bordered each other. It was damaged by fire *c.* 1914, but remained standing until the late 1930s. It was demolished in favour of the housing development of Holtwood.

H. L. C. Brassey was fond of horse-racing. He was an established breeder of fine stock. He registered his colours for the first time in 1893 and was elected a member of the Jockey Club in May 1898. He served as a Steward in 1901, 1903, 1908, 1935, 1936 and 1937. His trainer at Newmarket, T. Jenning Junior, produced winners of first-class races. The stud farm, established in 1895, lay to the north-east of the estate. It was a common sight to see the noble animals grazing in the paddock.

The stud groom's lodge, since named Little Preston Lodge, remained unaltered since Brassey's day. The brick walls were whitened. Over the wall surface at upper storey level were timbers in Elizabethan style. There were two upper storey oriel windows on the west. Two tall brick chimney stacks were original. The thatched roof was repaired in June 1980. The adjacent four-bay barn with centre gable survived. It was built in brick with a red tiled roof.

45

Chapter 9
THE DEVELOPMENT OF
A HOSPITAL COMPLEX

H. L. C. Brassey disposed of Preston Hall Estate *c.* 1906 by sale to Robert Horner of Spitalfields. The mansion remained unoccupied for some time. By 1907 Robert Sauber was in residence.

In 1914 the premises were requisitioned by the military authorities for use in hospitalising wounded troops brought home from the western front. The stud farm at Little Preston served as a veterinary and remount depot.

The estate was sold after 1918 by the widowed Madame Sauber. Home Farm was purchased by the sitting tenant Bert William Kemsley. The remainder of the estate, with the mansion, deer park and Holt Woods, was purchased by the Leeds Fireclay Company.

Industrial Settlements (Incorporated) purchased the estate, with the mansion, park, grounds, gardens, orchards, greenhouses, cottages and racquet court in *c.* 100 acres of land towards the end of 1919. A scheme was established in 1920 to open it as a training centre for tuberculous ex-Service men, mainly in country pursuits. The mansion was renovated and decorated. A central heating system and electric lighting were installed. A dining-room capable of seating 300 men was built on the south-east corner. Some 400 acres of land adjoining the estate were purchased.

The medical policy was simple and well defined. It aimed at providing rest and graduated exercise for patients suffering from tuberculosis. Workshops and a hostel were erected. Early enterprises included a carnation house in a horticultural department, cabinet-making, a pig farm, Angora stud for wool production, a poultry farm, gamekeeping and boot-making and repairing.

On the west of the inner door of the vestibule was a brass plaque recording the opening on 27 July 1921 by HRH Edward, Prince of Wales, of a colony for the treatment and training of tuberculous ex-Service men.

Opposite the main entrance on the south of the A20 stood a derelict property boarded up at the doors and windows. This was formerly the village stores, newsagent and post office at 203 London Road, given to the Preston Hall Colony in 1923 by The Empress Club Emergency Voluntary Aid Committee of 35 Dover Street, London. The Empress Club also provided the four bungalows on the north of Hermitage Lane. The task of providing further aid proved to be beyond the resources of the sponsors.

Mainly due to the efforts of Father Henry Aldersey, a former patient, a chapel alternative to the established Church of England was erected in 1923 on a slight eminence. It was dedicated to St Luke. Built in yellow and red brick with a red-tiled ridge roof of medium slope, it had a series of double doors along the south facade which facilitated fresh air for the tuberculosis patients. A bell-cote was tucked beneath the ridge of the west gable. The bell has disappeared.

Trefoil arched mullioned stone windows were in the west and east gables. Stained glass inserts in the east light portrayed John, Mark, Luke and Matthew. On the west gable, beneath a hood mould in the form of an equilateral obtuse pointed arch with return, was a four-light mullioned window. The central pair of lights were beneath acute pointed trefoil arches. The smaller flanking lights were beneath acute pointed trefoil arches with ogee geometric tracery. In these western lights were stained glass windows portraying Isaiah, Ezekiel, Jeremiah and Daniel.

Around the north and south internal walls were symbols representing the Stations of the Cross. Father Aldersey's death on 11 November 1924 was commemorated by a marble tablet on the south internal wall.

Industrial Settlements (Incorporated) ran into financial difficulties. Major General Sir Frederick Maurice KCMG, CB, the first elected Chairman of The British Legion, acquired at no cost, on 1 April 1925, the estate of Preston Hall. Included was the pioneer centre for the treatment, training and rehabilitation of ex-Service men suffering from pulmonary tuberculosis. There was a hospital of thirty-seven beds, with fifty-one patients in residence and thirty-six houses on the estate for ex-patients who had stayed after hospitalisation (called settlers) and their dependants. A portable building department provided occupational therapy and rehabilitation.

Dr P. C. Varrier-Jones MA, FRCP, who had achieved success at Papworth, Cambridgeshire in treating, training and rehabilitating sufferers from tuberculosis, was appointed the first medical superintendent. In 1926 Dr J. B. McDougall CBE, MD, FRCP (Ed), FRSE became the Medical Director. He was an enthusiastic amateur cricketer. Dr Varrier-Jones returned to his splendid work at Papworth and was later knighted.

The total population at Preston Hall in January 1926, comprising patients and their dependants, numbered 198. In the adjoining village were twenty-seven settlers.

In 1926 HRH Edward, Prince of Wales, made a visit. He became patron and took a keen personal interest in its activities. The project cultivated and captured royal interest which, by their inspiration and example, contributed materially to the success of the undertaking. The British Legion Press was established the same year. The following year a village hall was built on the south of the London Road and west of the Empress village stores. This became the Crescent Site. A training factory and housing accommodation improved the facilities.

With expanding industries and additional housing, the population increased to 467 by March 1928. George V (1910–36) visited The British Legion (BL) the same year. On 17 August the British Legion Disabled Men's Industries (Sales) Limited (BLI) suffered a major setback. In less than four hours, the entire carpentry department was destroyed by fire. The joinery workshop was consequently removed to a temporary cabinet-making workshop in the former badminton or racquet court north of the mansion. At the instigation of Sir Garrard Tyrwhitt-Drake, the Mayor of Maidstone, HRHs the Duke and Duchess of York visited Maidstone on 8 June 1929. The royal couple went on to visit The Legion's craft workshops and hospital at Preston Hall; this was followed by the presentation of a new standard to the local Legion branch at a ceremony in Mote Park. This was the year when the Advisory Council, a committee of nine settlers, was formed to act as representative of the settlers in all matters concerning the BLV.

In 1928 the Council of Management granted permission for the formation of a club in the village. The United Services Fund con-

The Artificial Lake and Boathouse in 1904

The Keeper's Cottage in 1904

The Holt on Richmond Hill in 1904

The Greenhouses to the north of the Hall in 1858

The Greenhouses in 1904

Above: The Bothy in 1904

Below: The Stud Groom's Lodge at Little Preston in 1904

Above: The Stables near Home Farm Cottage in 1904
Below: Ground Floor Plan in 1921

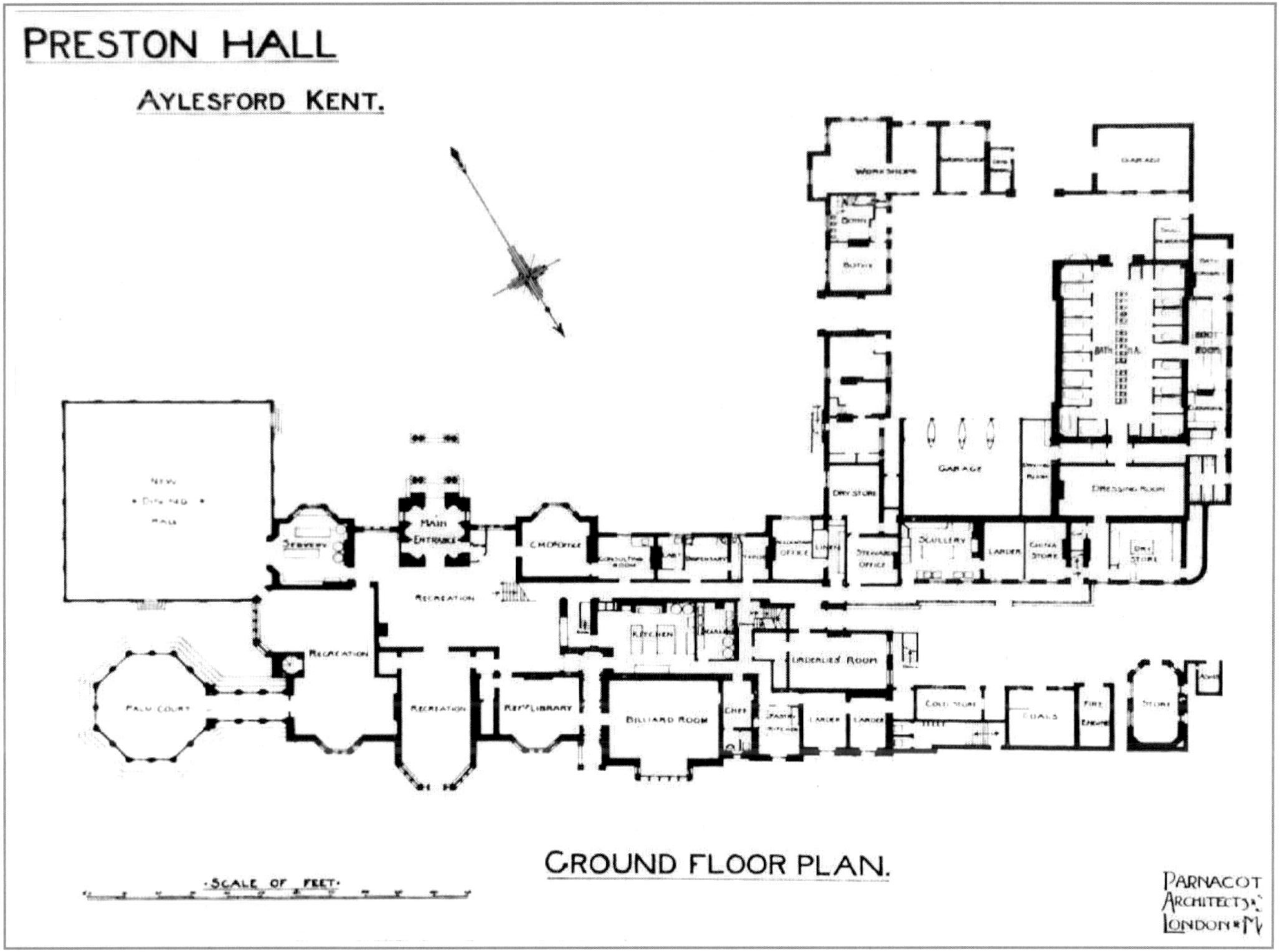

PRESTON HALL

AYLESFORD KENT.

GROUND FLOOR PLAN.

SCALE OF FEET.

PARNACOT
ARCHITECTS:
LONDON.

Labels within the plan:

GARAGE

WOMEN SHELTER

PANTRY

BUTLER

DRY STORE

SCULLERY

LARDER

DRESSING ROOM

GENERAL STORE

STEWARDS OFFICE

OFFICE

CHEF

KITCHEN

LAUNDRESS ROOM

CONSULTING

DUALS

FIRE ENGINE

AMBER LARDER

CONFC

BILLIARD ROOM

REFT. LIBRARY

CHEF OFFICE

MAIN ENTRANCE

RECREATION

RECREATION

RECREATION

NEW DINING HALL

PALM COURT

Visit of HRH Edward, Prince of Wales in 1932

The Empress Village Stores in 1949

St Ansano's Chapel in 1953

An internal view of St Ansano's Chapel in 1953

Part of the Crescent Site with the Village Hall in 1955

Above and below: Visit of HM Queen Elizabeth II on 5 December 1975

Aerial photograph of Preston Hall in 1950

tributed £225 towards material costs for the erection of the premises. The labour was provided by the settlers themselves in their spare time. The original building, formed of galvanised iron sheets on a timber frame, was sited adjoining the village hall on the Crescent Site south of the London Road. The Institute opened in May 1928 with a roll of eighty-six members.

Membership increased to 170, and accommodation became inadequate. The Medical Director mentioned this deficiency during a visit of Mr Capel Morris who immediately donated the sum of £600 towards the building of new club premises in memory of their late son Arthur. This new club, known as the 'Capel Morris British Legion Village Institute', opened in September 1936 at a cost of £1000. There were fifty-nine founder members surviving by 1939.

Arthur Capel Morris was born in Capel-le-Ferne, near Folkestone, Kent, in 1892. He resided at Norwood Hill, near Reigate, Surrey. He served as no. 4406 with the Lancers of the Line. He enlisted in London and, as Private Morris no. 6124, he was attached to the 1st Battalion, The Royal Munster Fusiliers. He was killed on active service in Gallipoli, the Dardanelles, on 27 November 1915. Consistent with those who have no known grave, his name was commemorated on the Helles Memorial. This was located at Cape Helles on the southwest tip of the Gallipoli Peninsula. The memorial register recorded his age as twenty-three years, the son of Mr and Mrs Capel Morris, of 78 The Drive, Hove, Sussex.

In 1930 Lieutenant Colonel G. R. Crosfield CBE, DSO, TD presented a 'hut' which was erected as a child welfare centre. It was located on the west of the main drive, north of the south lodge. Here, regular clinics were held and the appropriate preventative measures implemented. Dr J. B. McDougall reported in 1934 that no cases of tuberculosis meningitis had occurred among eighty-nine children who had been born in the village, and among the other juveniles none had contracted tuberculosis.

There was a school in which all children up to the age of nine years received elementary education.

A wood-graining department was established in the Industries in 1931. On 30 September 1931 there were 230 patients in residence, 555 people in the settlement itself, including 147 settlers, with a staff of 44. This presented a population of 829. There were 127 houses occupied by married settlers and two houses occupied by widows.

On 4 June 1932 HRH Edward, Prince of Wales, attended the Great Rally of The Kent British Legion at Preston Hall. The BLV Troop of Boy Scouts formed his guard of honour. He was escorted by Major General Sir F. Maurice, Chairman of The Legion.

There were 250 patients in residence in 1933. A café was erected.

Scientific advances in the treatment of tuberculosis involved an improvement in radiography and the extended use of collapse therapy, supplemented by major surgery. Such developments necessitated the building of an operating theatre which was completed in the Jellicoe Pavilion in 1933.

Laurence O'Shaunessy FRCS was a consultant here. He was a well-known thoracic surgeon and pioneer cardiac surgeon, who devised an operation for bringing the blood vessels to the heart from the abdomen. It was not very successful, but stimulated further attempts for improvement. His sister married Eric Blair (alias George Orwell). This led to Orwell's admission as a patient in 1939. L. O'Shaunessy remained on the staff until the war, when he joined the RAMC. His brilliant career ended when he was killed on active service in Flanders in 1940.

Douglas House, a convalescent home at Bournemouth, was acquired from the United Services Fund in 1934 as a seaside annexe to Preston Hall. There were seventy beds available at that time. This facility was further developed and extended. Patients benefited from the change from Preston Hall to Bournemouth, and vice versa.

HRHs the Duke and Duchess of Kent visited the BLV in 1935. The village Institute was extended. Dr J. B. McDougall, the Medical Director and Lieutenant Colonel G. R. Crosfield, Chairman of The BL visited Germany in 1935 and purchased an X-ray apparatus suitable for producing tomograms. This was the first instance of this application to be used in Britain. Except for an occasional tube replacement, the apparatus performed without breakdown until 1962 when it was replaced. The original apparatus passed to the Wellcome Medical Museum in London.

Tomography is the diagnostic radiological technique for obtaining clear X-ray images of deep internal structures by focusing on a specific plane within the body. This enabled the position of the tuberculosis lesions in the patient's chest to be accurately determined.

The Minister of Pensions, the Rt Hon. R. S. Hudson MP, visited The BL in 1936. HRH the Duchess of Kent visited the Industries informally the same year.

A grant from the National Executive Council of The BL enabled buildings in the hospital and industries to be altered extensively and modernised. A new hostel for the patients and a new factory for the fancy goods department were constructed by the settlers and completed early in 1939.

Chapter 10
PRESTON HALL AND
WORLD WAR TWO

With the outbreak of hostilities in 1939 the Emergency Medical Service opened a new general hospital on the estate. There were 360 beds available for the use of casualties in the event of an emergency. Together with the 150 sanatorium beds already existing, this was administered by The BL. Nearly 200 tuberculous patients already in Preston Hall were evacuated voluntarily in September. Some 100 patients remained, being unwilling to leave what they had come to regard as home. Additional medical, surgical, nursing and student staff were drafted from Guy's Hospital, London. A nurses' home was built to provide accommodation. By September 1940 some 2500 patients had been treated. Some 430 wounded troops from the Dunkirk beaches were admitted. Some 1800 sick and wounded Servicemen were treated. Some air-raid casualties were admitted. Between January and September 1940 over 700 operations were performed in the theatre.

The intensive Luftwaffe assault by aerial bombardment during 1940–1 resulted in no serious damage to the estate, and no loss of life.

Initially, each ward was identified by a number. They were later named in response to a request by the Friends of Preston Hall at a time when the hospital had ceased to expand and the incidence of tuberculosis was well into decline. Each ward was characterised by a local place name or its primary function (See the listing in Appendix 10.)

The development of facilities gradually evolved. Hostels, houses and factories were created to provide rehabilitation for tuberculous ex-Service men. Here, 35,000 such cases convalesced. By 1944 the total population at Preston Hall, comprising patients, settlers, dependants and staff, numbered 1641.

The title of The British Legion at Preston Hall was changed to the British Legion Industries (Preston Hall) Incorporated in 1944.

Dr Arnold Philip Bentley, MBE, MB, BS, completed his medical training at Charing Cross Hospital in 1945. He was appointed

Junior Medical Officer to The British Legion Hospital at Preston Hall, which cared for some 300 Service and ex-Service patients suffering from tuberculosis and ancillary heart and chest problems.

In 1945 Miss E. E. Hughes RRC, SRN, with a most distinguished war record, was appointed Chief Matron of Preston Hall, Douglas House and Nayland.

The granite cenotaph in the churchyard on the south of the church of St Peter and St Paul commemorated those who made the supreme sacrifice in World War Two. Servicemen who fell in the course of their duty were commemorated on the war memorial in Heaf Gardens. (Their names are recorded in Appendix 12.)

The fancy goods department, which had been abandoned due to the outbreak of hostilities in 1939, was opened on 3 July 1946 by the Rt Hon. George Isaacs MP, Minister of Labour and National Service.

Twenty prefabricated houses were erected in 1947 by Malling Rural District Council to accommodate the widows of settlers.

Chapter 11
THE POST-WAR YEARS

On 5 July 1948 the National Health Service was formed. The hospital wards, the nurses' home, Crosfield Pavilion and the mansion itself at Preston Hall were vested in the Ministry of Health under the South East Metropolitan Regional Hospital Board. The smaller units at Douglas House and Nayland were transferred to their respective Regional Hospital Board. The workshops, 110 houses in the village and most of the estate at Preston Hall remained the property of The BL. Some pavilions and chalets were shared. The BLV Training Scheme was inaugurated.

A line of poplar trees was planted in an east–west line across the north of the estate to provide a screen. Patients in the wards would no longer be distressed at the sight of funerals in Aylesford's cemetery.

Since the inception of hospital work at Preston Hall and the BLV, members of the Church of England were under the spiritual care of the vicar of Aylesford. The former riding-horse stable was converted into a memorial chapel. Some of the external ragstone masonry on the south was repaired with brickwork. Consecrated on 20 May 1949 by the Rt Rev C. M. Chavasse OBE, MC, DD, The Lord Bishop of Rochester, it was dedicated to St Ansano of Siena, the patron saint of chest diseases, in memory of Miss Elizabeth Lee ARRC. In May 1949 the Rev Gilbert Griffith-Thomas FRGS, Hon. CF, was publicly licensed as the first Resident Chaplain.

When the Industries celebrated their silver jubilee in 1950, there were 450 beds and 139 houses. Between 1925 and 1950, 10,000 patients benefited from the treatment.

The Hornsey Branch of The BL donated playing-field equipment for the children in the village. The presentation was made by Mr H. Worms of Hornsey on 1 October 1949. The Hancock Memorial Playground, donated by Essex County BL and located on the Crescent Site, opened in 1951. The John Young Memorial Hall (Youth Centre), located south of the Empress village stores and west of Hermitage Lane, opened in 1951.

HRHs the Duke and Duchess of Kent, and HRH. Princess Alexandra visited a BL County Rally at Preston Hall on 19 July 1953.

In 1954 a BLV 1939-45 memorial seat was unveiled.

In 1955 the Regional Hospital Board established the Public Health Laboratory Service.

The development of antibiotics during the 1950s was applied to the treatment of patients with tuberculosis. This enabled more rapid healing of a damaged lung. The incidence of the disease decreased to the extent that only one or two cases were under treatment at any one time. Patients were able to return to their own homes. The workforce of the Industries was depleted. The BL faced the possibility of closing down the Industries and the village. Dr A. P. Bentley, MBE, MB, BS, persuaded the Village Council to agree to his proposal to visit other units of sheltered employment. He voluntarily gave his annual leave for this project. He recommended that people with disabilities other than chest problems should be employed in the Industries. His report was subsequently studied by a working group. The Village Council and the National Executive Council of The BL accepted these proposals. The Industries continued to thrive.

A new central stores building for the works department was opened, and new lighting was installed in the fancy goods department in 1956. New presses were installed in the printing department in the Industries in 1958.

The Empress village stores, newsagent and post office at 203 London Road were modernised in 1957. This business was managed for many years by Len Watson. Bus shelters were erected outside the south perimeter wall, on the A20 road. The cost was shared between the Settlers, the Hospital Management Committee and the BLV Council.

A new oil-fired boiler was installed in 1958. A tall brick chimney on the west of the mansion provided the discharge of flue emissions well above the level of the top of the building.

The bronchitic unit opened in 1959. The Public Health Laboratory was erected by the Ministry of Health.

The Capel Morris BLV Institute extension was opened by Lieutenant Colonel Sir C. Gordon Larking CBE, FCA, the Chairman of the BL.

Land across the low-lying meadows north of the estate was acquired by the Kent County Council to construct a new motorway. During the summer of 1959 a vast bank of earth was raised. This became the M20 Maidstone by-pass, which opened in 1961.

A subway under the A20 road was completed by the Kent County Council in 1960. This provided safe access to pedestrians from the gates in the south perimeter wall to the Empress village stores.

The new boiler-house and a main kitchen in the hospital were completed in 1961. Four new cutters were installed in the carpentry department of the Industries in 1962.

Major Sir Brunel Cohen KBE, the first Chairman since 1948 of the Preston Hall Hospital Management Committee, resigned in 1963. O. A. Heaf Esq., MC, was appointed. New machines for The BL Press were purchased in 1963. Colonel W. Law OBE, MC, the General Manager of the BLI (1953–65), demonstrated the manufacture of Christmas crackers in the fancy goods department to HRH Princess Alice, Countess of Athlone, on her visit on 29 May 1963.

In 1963 the chapel was re-designed. The Caen stone roundels at the peak of the west and east gables were sealed with coursed ragstone. The wide doorways in the east gable and north facade were reduced by matching masonry and door surrounds. A new narrow iron-studded oak door in the east gable was presented by H. J. Colebrook of Fulmer, Bucks. Two double doors were provided in the north facade.

On the exterior masonry of the chapel above the entrance, formerly hung a ship's bell from HMS *Pembroke* at Chatham dockyard. The reredos was presented by West Malling church. The parish priest of St John's, Timberhill, Norwich, presented the altar ornaments. Lady Katrina Conway of Saltwood Castle, widow of a former owner of Allington Castle, presented a Flemish tapestry, through the good offices of Major Leslie Chalk, formerly Kent County Chairman of The BL. This delicate fabric, dating from *c.* 1550, depicted *Christ Descending from the Cross.* It hung on the north wall. It was removed to the reception area in the former atrium during 1979, and hung on the north wall above the entrance to the dining-room. By 1982 it was in store. Here, it suffered damage due to an infestation of rats.

A reading desk was a memorial to Miss Elizabeth Lee, a devoted nurse who was awarded the ARRC medal for the noble part she played in the Serbian retreat of 1915. She was Matron at Preston Hall in 1925–45. Her Christian life, manifested in character and service, impressed all who knew her.

On the south of the chapel a neglected garden was dominated by two tall stately conifer trees planted in the late 1950s. Here a sundial was dedicated to the life and work of Elizabeth Lee. Two Derbyshire stone memorial plaques commemorated two benefactors who had made possible the chapel alterations of 1963:

> Eveleen Dowling Kersley, born 18 August 1881 and died 22 March 1958.
> Rose Remmington, born 17 November 1881 and died 20 October 1961.

Several plaques mounted on the south ragstone wall commemorated:

> Martin William Twomey, a senior radiographer of Preston Hall, who died 13 May 1970.
> Mary Elizabeth Martin, Chairman, RBLV Women's Section, County Representative, and Founder of Village pre-school Play Group.

The Preston Hall Hospital Management Committee merged with the Mid-Kent Hospital Management Committee to form the Central Kent Hospital Management Committee in 1964.

The nurses' home was re-named Brunel Cohen House in July 1964 in memory of the late Major Sir Brunel Cohen KBE. He was a founder member of the BLV, the first Chairman of Preston Hall Hospital Management Committee, Treasurer of the BLV 1925–46, and President of the BLV 1945–65.

The reflective signs department of the Industries opened in 1964. At the close of 1964 the Industries employed 136 disabled persons, including 65 in various occupations in the hospital. The first edition in 1967 of Wilfred Pickles's popular radio show *Have a Go* was broadcast live from the BLV.

Poppies were initially made in this country in 1922 by five severely disabled ex-Servicemen, employed by the Disabled Society's Poppy Factory, working in a small room above a shop in

Bermondsey. This activity was founded by Major Howson. HRH Edward, Prince of Wales, suggested the need for the manufacture of poppy wreaths. The first wreath was placed by HRH the Prince of Wales on the Cenotaph on Armistice Day 11 November 1924.

Since 1926, some 40 million poppies were made annually on the site of an old brewery at The British Legion Poppy Factory Ltd., 20 Petersham Road, Richmond, Surrey. By 1933 a modern purpose-built factory replaced the former brewery which then served as a storage facility. For many years, poppies were distributed internationally from King's Cross, London.

To permit easier allocation, the distribution centre was moved in 1971 to Preston Hall. On the 60-acre estate of the BLV, some 1.25 acres on the site of the former pig farm became a new factory with a floor space of over 68,000 sq ft., and storage depot in 1972. Thousands of packaged poppies, crosses and wreaths were stored here for worldwide distribution prior to Remembrance Day.

The staff of forty local people included Joyce Inkpen, who was born in the village in 1928. Her father, Ernest Readman, was hospitalised at Preston Hall during World War One.

The prefix 'Royal' was bestowed on The British Legion on the occasion of its 50th Anniversary on 27 May 1971, by command of Her Gracious Majesty Queen Elizabeth II.

On 25 June 1971 HRH the Duchess of Kent opened the Duchess of Kent Court, which consisted of twenty-eight double flats and fourteen single flats. By 1972 the former workshops on the south-west of the estate were demolished to provide space for building new accommodation for ex-Servicemen. In 1974, 104 new dwellings were opened.

An important feature of the landscaped village was the one- and two-bedroom flats and three-bedroom houses, provided for more than 500 ex-Service men and their families, including some eighty houses occupied by factory personnel. A new hostel block was completed in 1973. It was named Dennis Cadman Court after a former National Vice-Chairman of The RBL. It had forty-four two-roomed flats replacing temporary chalets which had outlived their usefulness.

On the retirement of the Rev G. Griffith-Thomas in 1974, the chapel lapsed into desuetude, and became a store. It was later converted for use as a lecture room. The spiritual care of the community returned to the incumbent of Aylesford. The Rev Griffith-Thomas (1907–77) was interred in the north-west of the churchyard of the parish church.

Hundreds of local school children had leave of absence on 5 December 1975 when HM Queen Elizabeth II, in a fur-collared coat with matching hat, visited the RBLV as part of its 50th anniversary celebrations. Accompanied both by Mr T. S. C. Busby, CBE, AE, FSVA, DL, Chairman of The RBL, and the Chairman of Tonbridge and Malling District Council, the Queen informally visited the poppy warehouse, the fancy goods warehouse, and the signs department. She met and chatted with some elderly people, officials and disabled workers, including the village's oldest inhabitant, Mrs Elsie Taylor, a resident for the entire fifty years. Standard bearers of The Kent Branch of The RBL formed a guard of honour as Her Majesty left the village. A plaque on the south wall of the offices of the poppy warehouse commemorated Her Majesty's visit.

A new and taller chimney stack was erected above the boiler house in 1979. By increasing the height of the stack, oxides of sulphur were dispersed to avoid damaging the soft alkaline masonry.

A small residential cul-de-sac named Clark Mews was created to the north-west of the mansion, on the site of the former kitchen garden. On the south of the former perimeter wall of yellow brick, adorned with climbing roses, was the well-maintained Heaf Gardens. Randomly planted across a green sward were a variety of flowering trees and shrubs. Surrounded by a prolific border of tulips, polyanthus, daffodils and wallflowers was a random ragstone memorial commemorating the fallen of World War Two. A flowering cherry tree was planted by HRH the Duchess of Kent when she opened this garden on 13 May 1980.

Until 1973 only cases requiring thoracic surgery were admitted to Preston Hall Hospital. The treatment of other chest complaints was gradually undertaken. By 1982, this was the only hospital in Kent involved with thoracic surgery. The buildings, almost all of which were made of wood, were falling into disrepair.

The number of chest patients decreased. Consequently, there was an increase in General Medicine. There were two Consultant Physicians specialising in Chest Diseases, and two specialising in General Medicine, in addition to the Thoracic Surgery and Cardiology. A second operating theatre was provided, which enabled the introduction of General Surgery and Orthopaedic Surgery in 1973. Gynaecology followed in June 1981.

In addition to Thoracic Surgery, by 1982 there were two Consultant Orthopaedic Surgeons, two Consultant General Surgeons and a Consultant Gynaecologist operating in the two theatres.

By 1982 this was the sole Intensive Therapy Unit in the Maidstone District, with a spectacular record of success in treating serious chest injuries and seriously ill patients.

There was an 'Extravaganza' gala on May bank holiday 29–30 May 1982. There were arena displays by The Western Saddle Club, The Manor Corps of Drums, The Americanettes Majorettes and the Maids of Kent Majorettes. With stalls and refreshments to cater for a host of visitors in the grounds, it proved to be a successful fund-raising venture for Preston Hall Hospital.

The Churchill Rehabilitation and Assessment Centre was erected to the east of the former Elizabeth Lee Pavilion and completed in 1982 to commemorate The RBL's 60th anniversary and the International Year of Disabled Persons. The single-storied brick-built structure with shallow sloping roof was owned by The RBL on land leased from the RBLI. The Centre was administered by a Trust with members drawn from The RBL and the Health Authority. The construction of the Centre was to a very high standard, incorporating the latest technology, with particular attention paid to the needs of disabled people. Excellent facilities were offered for the treatment and rehabilitation of the disabled. Included was a physiotherapy department with a comprehensive range of equipment comprising electrotherapy treatment, including short wave, interferential treatment, laser therapy and ultrasound treatment. There was also a hydrotherapy pool and a gymnasium, together with a well-equipped occupational therapy department.

Disabled ex-Service personnel were accepted for courses of treatment to overcome or diminish their disability. Staff were employed both by The RBL and the Health Authority. Dr A. P. Bentley, MBE, MB, BS, on retirement from the National Health Service in 1986, became the Medical Consultant until February 1995. Both National Health Service and The RBL sponsored patients were admitted. It was intended to serve both the local community and ex-Service patients from all parts of the United Kingdom.

In 1983 the offices in the mansion at Preston Hall became the headquarters of the Maidstone Health Authority.

The Maidstone General Hospital opened for receiving patients in October 1983, just over three years after building work began. It consolidated in one unit the health services which hitherto had been scattered in three separate hospitals, viz. the West Kent General, Fant Lane and Preston Hall. The Maidstone Hospital was officially opened by HRH Princess Alexandra on 4 June 1984.

The function of Preston Hall started to change. Good medical practice dictated concentration of effort at Maidstone. Various functions were transferred. The kitchen and most of the wards were closed in 1987 because the corresponding facilities at Maidstone were superior. Remaining at Preston Hall were an operating theatre, three wards for the treatment of in-patients, the X-ray and cardio-respiratory departments, the outpatient clinics for orthopaedics, chest medicine and genito-urinary medicine, and the microbiology and histopathology laboratories.

Because of loss of part of the roof at Oakwood Hospital during the hurricane-force storm of 16 October 1987, some thirty psychiatric patients were hastily transferred into the disused Allington ward at Preston Hall. Here they remained for some nine months.

The Capel Morris RBLV Institute club moved from the Crescent Site on 7 August 1988, to the Essie Harris Pavilion, which was an obsolete wooden hospital building. The former building on the Crescent Site was cleared by fire. The houses were demolished. The site was purchased and occupied by the supermarket of J. Sainsbury plc at Mills Road, Quarrywood Industrial Estate.

The subway under the A20 road was filled in during the widening of the road in 1988–9.

The new architect-designed Community Centre and Capel Morris Club house was adjacent to Hall Road. It was a red-brick building with a steeply sloping roof of matching red tiles. It opened on 22 August 1990, with some 250 people attending.

Brian K. Sharp was appointed Club Steward in September 1987. He was promoted to Manager at the inception of the new premises. He left in June 1995.

The Heart of Kent Hospice was built to the east of the estate on the north-east corner of St Luke's Chapel. The foundation stone was laid on 12 July 1990 by Countess Mountbatten of Burma. In landscaped grounds, the hospice was designed by the architect Colin Albin in yellow and red brick under a slate roof of medium slope. Fund-raising started in 1985 with the Wishing Well Appeal. The hospice was built by the Maidstone Hospice Appeal, which was founded on 27 October 1987. The name was changed on 19 February 1992 to the Heart of Kent Hospice. This registered charity (Registered Charity No. 298164) is devoted to maintaining the hospice.

St Luke's Chapel was converted into the Hospice Chapel. The former double doors along the south facade were replaced by modern windows in wooden frames. The altar, traditionally at the east, was replaced by a new simple altar on the west. This facilitated access by bed-ridden patients from the Hospice. An oak reading desk commemorated Martin William Twomey.

The Rev Paul Francis was appointed the first Chaplain in 1991. Due to the pressures of his parochial commitments, he was unable to afford the level of attention which was necessary. Donald Bish, retired as Rector of Wateringbury, Teston and West Farleigh on 31 May 1992, was requested by the Bishop of Tonbridge to take up the responsibility as Chaplain.

The Heart of Kent Hospice was designed to cater for up to fifty day care patients a week with beds for ten in-patients at a time. It offered a flexible service which patients used as the need arose. It opened on 28 October 1991 to provide specialised palliative care for patients suffering from advanced disease who no longer received treatment with a curative focus. Using an holistic approach with the latest methods of symptom and pain control, and by catering for the patient's emotional, spiritual and social needs, the hospice attempted to relieve pain, fear and loneliness.

The hospice's patron was Marianna, Viscountess Monckton of Brenchley. HRH Diana, Princess of Wales, officially opened the hospice on 21 October 1992. She unveiled a plaque near the entrance. The Princess met all the patients, relatives, staff and the many supporters who had worked so diligently to make the day possible.

The staff and function of the hospice were featured on the 'Regional News Magazine' programme broadcast by ITV Meridian on 21 June 1995.

Adjacent to the Capel Morris Club house was the Gordon Larking Community Centre. It was opened by HRH the Duchess of Kent on 17 September 1992. A plaque over the inner door of the lobby of the Capel Morris Club house commemorated the occasion.

The Prince Philip Lodge, in yellow brick with stone mullioned windows and tiled roof, was built in 1992. This small attractive block of self-contained flats was managed by the British Commonwealth Ex-Services League who decided who was accommodated here. Precedence was given to ex-Service and expatriate personnel who were forced by conflict to leave their homes in Africa.

Gavin Astor House nursing home was built on the site of the former Essie Harris Pavilion. The foundation stone was laid on 21 July 1992 by the Lord Lieutenant of Kent, the Rt Hon. Robin Leigh-Pemberton. This nursing home was dedicated to the memory of Gavin Astor, 2nd Lord Astor of Hever K. St. J., Lord Lieutenant of Kent 1972–82, in appreciation of the great service which he gave to the RBLI over many years both as benefactor and as president. The building cost was met from the sale of the Crescent Site which was occupied by the supermarket of J. Sainsbury plc.

The two-storied brick-built Gavin Astor House, with tiled roof, opened in September 1993 to receive patients. The official opening was on 4 July 1994. The Lord Lieutenant of Kent, the Rt Hon. Lord Kingsdown, KG, PC, officiated at a ceremony which attracted about 150 people. This thirty-three-bed facility was intended to serve both the local community and ex-Service personnel. Gavin Astor House is part of a registered charity (Registered Charity No. 210063).

The fabric of Preston Hall roof was restored in 1992–4. New roof slates and chimney stacks, with new fascias and cladding, in congruent style to the original, were urgently needed to prevent the ingress of rainwater. Probably at this time the flagstaff and weather vane were removed from the top of the central tower.

The building contractor Charles Walter commenced extensive restorations on the south gate lodge in September 1994. Main drainage was fitted. Most of the timber suffered from dry rot and was replaced. All the internal walls were plastered. A reinforced concrete floor secured against rising damp. Purbeck limestone replaced the eroded Kentish ragstone. The Caen stone quoins and window surrounds were replaced in Cadeby limestone. This type of material was used in the restoration of York Minster. New slates were applied to the existing timber roof. The chimney stack was rebuilt in brick. An inglenook fireplace in the centre of the building was restored to its original splendour. The work was completed by March 1995.

A workforce of some 129 people, most of whom were disabled, were employed in the RBLI *c.* 1994. This subsidised concern of The RBL was developed under one roof in a spacious factory containing such commercial activities as superb printers producing letterpress and lithographic work for leaflets and colour brochures, timber pallet manufacture, with the manufacture of traffic signs in a variety of materials for use on road and rail to provide directions. High-quality precision engraving presented top quality logos or names on a variety of materials. Medical guidance to people with disabilities in Kent was developed by an Occupational Health Department. The Industries is part of a registered charity called the Royal British Legion Industries (Preston Hall) Incorporated (Registered Charity No. 210063).

The domestic heating of the mansion was converted to a gas-fired system. Two new boilers were located in a vacant basement room accessed from the tunnel. The obsolete boiler house was demolished in December 1994 and January 1995 to facilitate the installation of a brick-paved car-park.

The West Kent Health Authority was formed in 1994 by the merger of four smaller authorities, viz. Dartford & Gravesham, Medway, Maidstone and Tunbridge Wells. The headquarters were in the mansion at Preston Hall.

Business was conducted through a board whose collective duty was to initiate the strategic direction for health care locally, to allocate funds, monitor health care and influence improvements in public health.

With a staff of 135, on a budget of £357 million for 1994/5, and £365 million for 1995/6, the Authority purchased NHS hospital and community care and treatment for a population of 950,000 in the district between Dartford and Sittingbourne in the north to Edenbridge and Hawkhurst in the south. In 1996 the Authority accepted responsibility for administering the functions of general practitioners, dentists, pharmacists and opticians. To support this object, the budget was raised to a sum over £500 million.

Considerable efforts were made in developing the role of the new Authority in planning and securing the provision of health services for the residents of West Kent. Links were forged between General Practitioners, Community Health Councils, Kent County Council Social Services and Education departments, local Borough, District and City Councils who were responsible for the environment, housing and leisure, together with other organisations concerned with health and health care.

The objective was to develop a comprehensive health strategy initiating priorities for the next five to ten years, to apply funds to these priorities and monitor progress and achievements as a result of the investment.

The beginning of 1996 saw extensive building operations within and around the mansion of Preston Hall. The main reception area was completely upgraded. A new partition wall was fitted in the east. The existing doors were refurbished and stained dark oak and varnished. New brass handles were fitted to the doors. The internal walls were redecorated. A new carpet was fitted and the existing reception desk was replaced with an improved model. The artificial lighting was improved and massive wall radiators applied heating to areas where previously there had been none.

An additional door in mahogany and glass was fitted under the arch of the vestibule into the reception area. The style of the changes was congruent to the existing image.

The two collapsed masonry pillars on either side of the approach before the south porch were restored to their former glory by a specialist firm of contractors. To facilitate the passage of vehicular traffic, the pillars were set further apart than formerly.

The car-park to the east of Brunel Cohen House was extended north and south and surfaced with blue brick on a bed of fine sand.

These innovations were necessary to implement the function of the mansion and to safeguard the fabric well into the next century. On an annual budget in 1996 of £500 million, this administration centre was maintained as a caring site to protect the health care of almost one million local people.

The day-care facilities of the Heart of Kent Hospice were enhanced by building an extension. This provided a hairdressing salon to include beauty treatment, additional offices, storage facilities and a family or children's room. Grants of £400,000 provided for the building costs, without encroaching on the funds available for the running costs. The 'Children in Need' charity funded c. £5,500 towards the purchase of furniture for the family room. The services available in the hospice were improved by including reminiscence therapy and various alternative therapies. There was no increase in capacity for in-patients.

The builders E. C. Gransden & Co Ltd of Upchurch started work on 19 September 1995 by clearing the former garden on the east for the new foundations. The former east gable was removed. The style of architecture and the selection of building materials was similar to that of the earlier fabric. Below the new east gable a patio was created in granite setts on a foundation of sand.

The work was completed by 28 March 1996. Some 300 full-time and voluntary staff attended the official opening by Councillor Pat Barnes on 3 May 1996.

The history of Preston Hall is a record of progressive development initiated by changes in function. Over the years many residents have exerted their influence on the local fabric and community before passing on to the inevitable higher calling. Their memory fades into the mists of time. But the product of their labours is an achievement, constituting our sacred heritage which we maintain for the next generation.

Appendix 1
THE AYLESFORD BRANCH OF THE CULPEPPER FAMILY

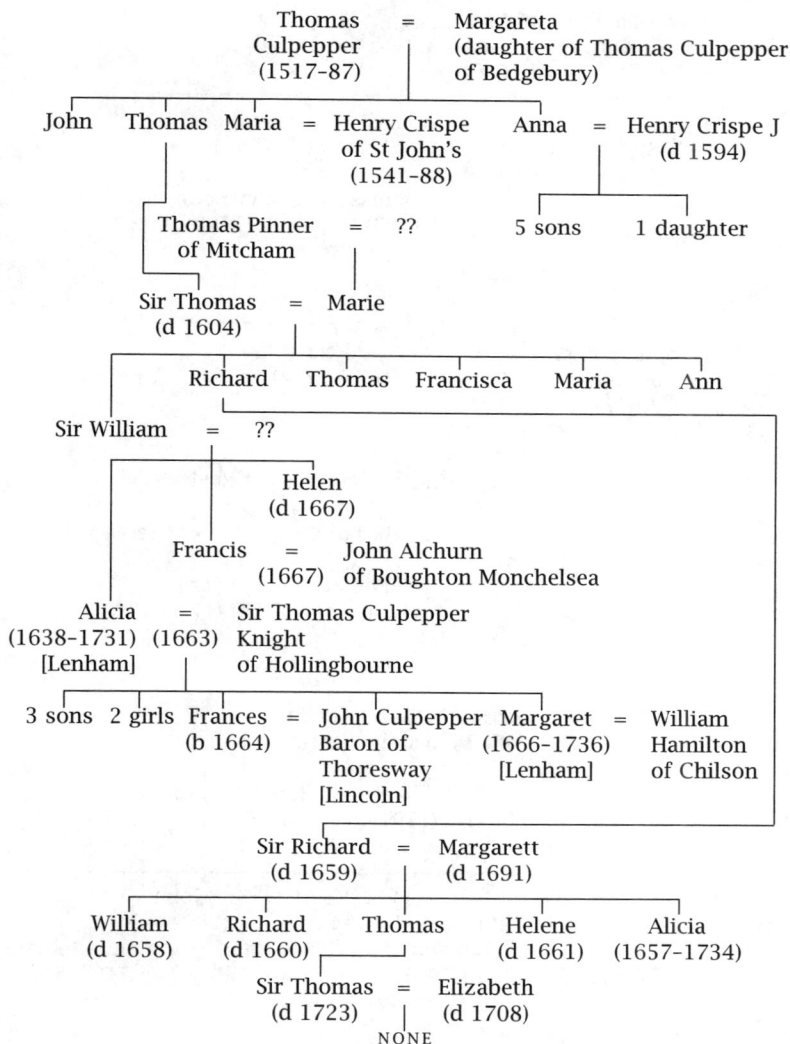

Thomas Culpepper (1517-87) = Margareta (daughter of Thomas Culpepper of Bedgebury)

Children of Thomas Culpepper and Margareta:
- John
- Thomas
- Maria = Henry Crispe of St John's (1541-88)
- Anna = Henry Crispe J (d 1594)
  - 5 sons
  - 1 daughter

Thomas Pinner of Mitcham = ??

Sir Thomas (d 1604) = Marie
- Richard
- Thomas
- Francisca
- Maria
- Ann

Sir William = ??
- Helen (d 1667)
- Francis = John Alchurn (1667) of Boughton Monchelsea
- Alicia (1638-1731) [Lenham] = (1663) Sir Thomas Culpepper Knight of Hollingbourne
  - 3 sons
  - 2 girls
  - Frances (b 1664) = John Culpepper Baron of Thoresway [Lincoln]
  - Margaret (1666-1736) [Lenham] = William Hamilton of Chilson

Sir Richard (d 1659) = Margarett (d 1691)
- William (d 1658)
- Richard (d 1660)
- Thomas
- Helene (d 1661)
- Alicia (1657-1734)

Sir Thomas (d 1723) = Elizabeth (d 1708)

NONE

67

Appendix 2

THE AYLESFORD BRANCH OF
THE MILNER FAMILY

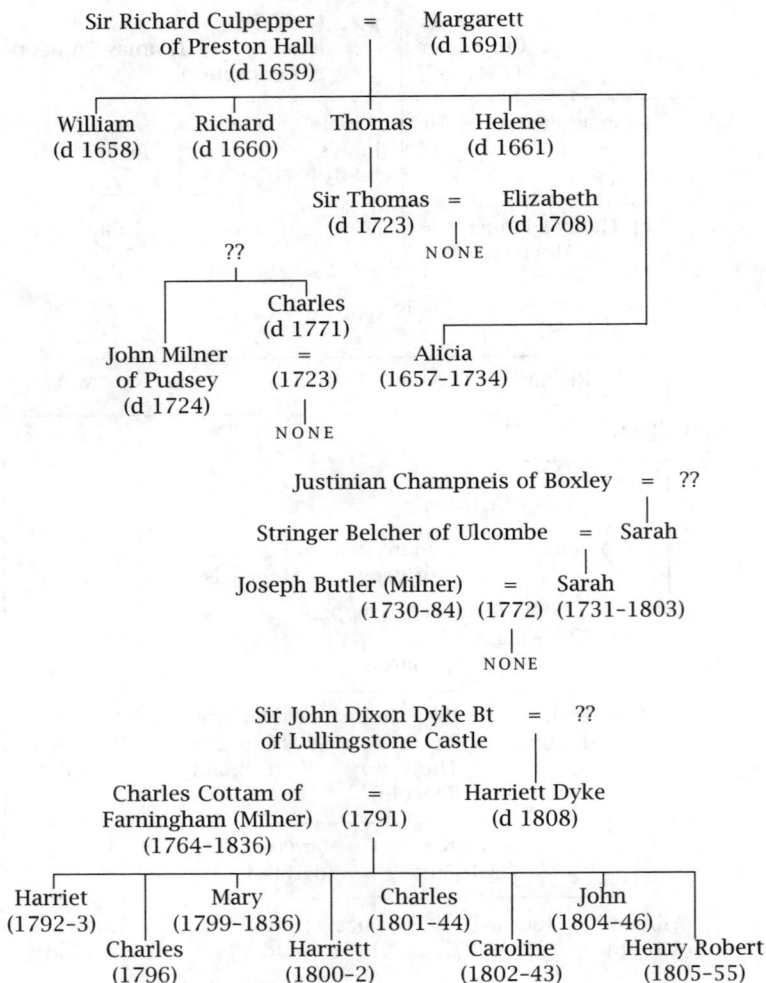

Sir Richard Culpepper = Margarett
of Preston Hall   (d 1691)
(d 1659)

William   Richard   Thomas   Helene
(d 1658)   (d 1660)   (d 1661)

Sir Thomas = Elizabeth
(d 1723)   (d 1708)
            NONE

??

Charles
(d 1771)

John Milner   =   Alicia
of Pudsey   (1723)   (1657-1734)
(d 1724)
            NONE

Justinian Champneis of Boxley = ??

Stringer Belcher of Ulcombe = Sarah

Joseph Butler (Milner)   =   Sarah
(1730-84) (1772) (1731-1803)
                NONE

Sir John Dixon Dyke Bt = ??
of Lullingstone Castle

Charles Cottam of   =   Harriett Dyke
Farningham (Milner)   (1791)   (d 1808)
(1764-1836)

Harriet   Mary   Charles   John
(1792-3)   (1799-1836)   (1801-44)   (1804-46)
       Charles   Harriett   Caroline   Henry Robert
       (1796)   (1800-2)   (1802-43)   (1805-55)

DIMENSIONS OF THE CULPEPPER MONUMENT
IN THE CHURCH OF ST PETER AND ST PAUL AT AYLESFORD

Dimension	Value ft in	
Height of the cornice above the chancel floor	3	11
Maximum height above the chancel floor	5	9
Maximum length, measured at the architrave	6	4
Maximum width, measured at the architrave	4	2
Maximum length, measured at the lower plinth	6	1.5
Maximum width, measured at the lower plinth	4	4.5
Length of the male effigy	5	7
Length of the female effigy	5	5

Appendix 4
THE AYLESFORD BRANCH OF
THE BETTS FAMILY

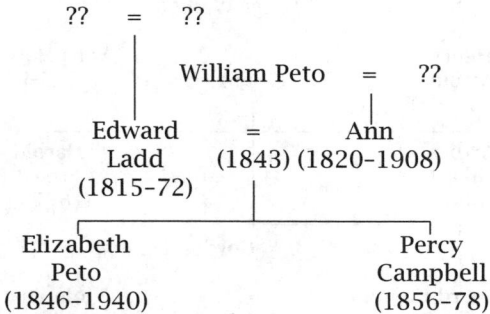

```
        ??    =    ??
              |
              |      William Peto    =    ??
              |                           |
           Edward        =        Ann
            Ladd      (1843)  (1820–1908)
          (1815–72)              |
      _____
      |                                      |
   Elizabeth                              Percy
     Peto                                Campbell
  (1846–1940)                           (1856–78)
```

THE AYLESFORD BRANCH OF
THE BRASSEY FAMILY

```
John Brassey        =        ??
  of Bulkeley
        |
        |                Joseph Harrison    =    ??
        |                  of Birkenhead
        |                        |
        Thomas       =       Maria
      (1805-70)    (1831)
        |
    ┌──────────────────────────────────────┐
   John                                  Albert
    |                                       |
 Thomas (1)      =      Anna Allnutt        |
 (1836-1918)  (1860)    (d 1887)            |
    |                                       |
 ┌───────┬──────────┬──────────┬──────────┐│
 son   daughter  daughter   daughter  daughter
                                            |
            Viscount Malden   =   ??        |
                   |                        |
 Thomas (2)    =   Sybil de Vere Capell     |
 (1836-1918) remarried                      |
          (1890)                            |
    |                                       |
 daughter                                   |
                                            |
    ┌───────────────────────────────────────┘
    |        George Robert Stevenson    =    ??
    |           of Tongs Wood
    |                 |
  Henry        =      Anna Harriet
  Arthur    (1866)    (1845-98)
 (1840-91)           |
    |                |
  Arthur          Harold
  Albert          Ernest
 (1868-9)        (1877-?)
    |
    |              Gordon-Lennox    =    ??
    |                    |
 Henry Leonard Campbell  =   Violet Mary
 (1870-1958)          (1894) (d 1946)
    |
 ┌────────┬────────┬────────┬────────┬────────┐
 Ronald  Cecil   Gerald    John   Bernard  Peter
 Henry   Henry   Charles  Leonard Thomas   Esme
 (1895) (1896-  (1898-   (1903)  (1905-67)(1907-?)
        1949)    1918)
```

Appendix 6

LIST OF PAINTINGS IN PRESTON HALL
AT THE CLOSE OF THE 19TH CENTURY

PAINTER	TITLE
V. Bartholomew (1799–1879)	*Flowers*
C. W. Cope (1811–90)	*The Marriage of Griselda*, 1852
T. Creswick (1811–69)	*A Roadside Inn*
A. Cuyp (1605–91)	*Cavaliers*
A. Cuyp	*Houses*
L. Haghe (1806–85)	*Michaelangelo*, in watercolour
L. Haghe	*An Interior*, in watercolour
G. Lance (1802–64)	*A Fruit Piece,* in oils
Sir E. H. Landseer (1802–73)	*A Morning on Braemar*
D. Maclise (1811–70)	*The wrestling scene from 'As You Like It'*, introducing the park front of Preston Hall, 1855
D. Maclise	*A Sketch*
A. van Ostade (1610-85)	*An Interior, with boars drinking*
W. C. Stanfield (1793-1867)	*The Fort and Harbour of Rochelle*, 1851
D. Teniers (1610–94)	*A Drinking and Singing Party*
D. Teniers	*Obelisk*
F. W. Topham (1808–77)	*Mavourneen*, an Irish subject
F. W. Topham	*Cushla Machree*, an Irish subject
E. H. Wenhert (1813–68)	*Murillo*
J. Wijants (1615–79)	*Travellers Attacked*
J. Wijants	*A Landscape*

Note: There were many family portraits around the mansion. Above the marble fireplace in the dining-room in 1886 were portraits of Sir Morton Peto and E. L. Betts on either side of a portrait of an elegant lady and child. This may have been Betts's wife Ann and daughter Elizabeth.

Appendix 7
CONTRACTORS AND SUPPLIERS TO INDUSTRIAL SETTLEMENTS (INCORPORATED)

James Armstrong & Co. Ltd., 116 Queen Victoria Street, London. Supplied and fitted equipment for the laundry, including a water softening plant and sterilising apparatus.

Benham & Son, Wigmore Street, London. Installed domestic water and water heating facility.

Mr A. C. Brown, Aylesford. Supplied the poultry houses and the fittings.

Cox Bros., Builders, Maidstone. Erected eight cottages and a bungalow for the occupation of instructors and departmental heads.

Hobman & Co., South Bermondsey. Laid the asphalt paths to the huts and the drive to the mansion.

Oswald Jones & Co., Maidstone. Installed electric supply to the huts, sanitary block, orderlies' quarters and the laundry.

Keith, Blackman & Co., Farringdon Avenue, London. Provided ventilation to the lavatories, etc.

McDowall, Steven & Co., 2 Upper Thames Street, London. Supplied and installed steam cooking equipment.

Mr C. H. Nunn, Gypsy Hill, London, and Riley & Co., of Herne Hill, London. Supplied the specially made huts (single and double) for the open-air treatment of patients.

Parnacott's, 93 York Road, London and Broadway, Maidstone. This firm of architects and surveyors prepared the specifications, plans and supervised the entire building work.

Parry & Son, Old Street, London. Supplied the cabinet-makers' benches.

Pinchin & Walton, Cannon Street, London. Installed electric supply to the mansion.

Roneo Ltd., Holborn, London. Supplied the metal lockers for the patients' use.

Tyzack & Son, Old Street, London. Supplied the cabinet-making tools for the workshops.

G. E. Wallis & Sons Ltd. Contractors, Broadmead Works, Maidstone. Completed the alterations and improvements to the mansion, laundry and outbuildings, constructed the orderlies' quarters, sick bay and the sanitary block.

Appendix 8
MEDICAL DIRECTORS OF THE
ROYAL BRITISH LEGION AND INDUSTRIES

Date	Director
1925-6	Sir Pendrill C. Varrier-Jones, MA, MRCS, FRCP
1926-44	Dr J. B. McDougall CBE, MD, FRCP, FRS, (Ed)
1944-8	Professor F. R. G. Heaf CMG, MA, MD, FRCP
1948-72	Dr F. Temple Clive MB, BS

Appendix 9
CHAIRMEN OF THE ROYAL BRITISH LEGION

Date	Chairman
1925-9	Major General Sir Frederick Maurice KCMG, CB
1930-5	Lieutenant Colonel G. R. Crosfield CBE, DSO, TD
1936-65	Lieutenant Colonel Sir C. Gordon Larking CBE, FCA
1965-	T. S. C. Busby CBE, AE, FSVA, DL

Appendix 10
WARDS IN PRESTON HALL HOSPITAL

12	Kits Coty Ward.
9	Holt Wood Ward.
7	Forstal Ward, which later became Operating Theatre 2.
5	Ditton Ward. 'Solaria' lounge and public telephone.
3	Birling Ward.
2	Allington Ward.
4	Cobtree Ward.
6	Eccles Ward, and Intensive Treatment Unit.
8	X-ray Department.
11	Operating Theatre 1.
10	Out-patients Department and Cardio Respiratory Laboratory.
13	Larkfield Ward.
14	Physiotherapy and Occupational Therapy.
15	Elizabeth Lee Ward.
16	Community Education Centre.
17	District Laboratory.
18	Public Health Laboratory.

Note: The listing started with the south-west corner.

Appendix 11
PAVILIONS, HOSTELS, COURTS AND LODGES BUILT BY THE ROYAL BRITISH LEGION

Date Completed	Facility	Date Demolished
1925	New hostel erected, renamed Essie Harris Pavilion in 1952.	1991
1926	25 houses in the Crescent built.	
1927	Village Hall built.	
1927	28 houses in London Road East built.	
1928	12 houses in East Park Road built.	
1928	4 houses built under British Legion Area Housing Scheme.	
1930	British Legion Village Institute opened, renamed Capel Morris.	
1930	Crosfield hut erected.	
1933	Jellicoe Pavilion opened.	
1938	Crosfield Pavilion erected.	1988–90
1939	Orchard Pavilion erected.	
1939	Nurses' home erected, renamed Brunel Cohen House in 1964.	
1947	20 prefabricated houses erected.	
1951	John Young Memorial Hall (Youth Centre) opened.	
1952	Gordon Larking Pavilion completed.	1988–90
1955	23 Gordon Larking chalets opened.	
1956	11 Gordon Larking chalets opened.	
	Elizabeth Lee Pavilion.	1988–90
	Charles Busby Court.	
	Earl Haig.	
	Lord Allenby.	
1970	Duchess of Kent Court.	
1973	Dennis Cadman Court.	
1982	Churchill Rehabilitation Centre.	
1985	Mountbatten Pavilion.	
1992	Prince Philip Lodge built.	

1993   Gavin Astor House opened.

Note: These buildings were named after benefactors to The Royal British Legion.

Ground Plan of the Royal British Legion Village in 1995.
By the courtesy of the Royal British Legion Industries.

Appendix 12
'WE WILL REMEMBER THEM'

Recorded on the granite cenotaph in the church yard on the south of the church of St Peter and St Paul are those who made the supreme sacrifice in World War Two:

Frederick James Bearman, DCM.
Geoffrey William Danes.
Charles William Ronald Dean.
Jack Lancelot Phillips.
Raymond Thomas Phillips.
Harry Douglas Poole.

Recorded on the war memorial in Heaf Gardens, on the north-west of Preston Hall are those who made the supreme sacrifice in World War Two:

Edwin Collins, Sgt, RAFVR.
Alfred C. Hurley, LAC, RAFVR.
David M. Love, MM Sgt, R. Ulster Rifles
James Sparrow, F/Sgt, RAF.
Albert Stevens, Pte, LDV.
Michael M. Watson, P/O, RAFVR.

Appendix 13
POEM 'IN FLANDERS' FIELDS'

In Flanders' Fields the poppies blow
    Between the crosses, row on row,
That mark our place; and in the sky
    The larks, still bravely singing fly
Scarce heard amid the guns below.

We are the dead. Short days ago
    We lived, felt dawn, saw sunset glow,
Loved and were loved, and now we lie
    In Flanders' fields.

Take up our quarrel with the foe;
    To you from failing hands we throw
The torch; be yours to hold it high.
    If ye break faith with us who die
We shall not sleep, though poppies grow
    In Flanders' fields.

Note: It was Colonel John McCrae, a well known Professor of Medicine at the Canadian University of McGill, who first wrote of the Flanders Poppy as the 'Flower of Remembrance'. He served in France with the first Canadian contingent as a Medical Officer. He wrote these verses in a small first-aid post at the second battle of Ypres in 1916. He died in May 1918, and was interred in a cemetery above Wimereux.

"The Story of the Poppy", **The Emblem**, 12, 1956, No 11, October, pp 8-11.

SELECT BIBLIOGRAPHY

A. Brown, 'The Royal British Legion Village 60th Anniversary 1925-1985', 1985

C. Busby, 'A New Era has Dawned', 'The Royal British Legion Village 50th Anniversary 1925-75', 1977, pp. 7-9

F. Temple Clive, *A Brief Medical History of Preston Hall, 1925-1965*, 1965

S. Denne, 'Inscriptions on a Barn Door near Preston Hall' in *Archaeologia 13*, 1800, pp. 107-40

J. Ingle, *Preston Hall – History and Legend*, 1977

J. B. McDougall, *Report of the Medical Director*, 1944

A. Leland Noel, *Home Counties Magazine 11*, 1909, pp. 32-8

J. H. Sephton, 'The Culpepper Monument in St Peter's Church Aylesford', *Aylesford Contact*, May 1980, p. 5

S. Wagon, 'The Charities of Aylesford', 1913

S. Wagon, 'Record of Matters Relating to Aylesford Church', 1918

K. A. E. Wells, 'The Brassey Family and Preston Hall', 1979

K. A. E. Wells, 'Preston Hall and its Owners', 1985

G. Wootton, *The Official History of The British Legion,* 1956